RESTORING Love

Ruth
It Sets Us Free!
[signature]

RESTORING Love

DEBBIE ALSDORF

For Her. For God. For Real.

Faithfulwoman.com

Faithful Woman is an imprint of
Cook Communications Ministries, Colorado Springs, Colorado 80918
Cook Communications, Paris, Ontario
Kingsway Communications, Eastbourne, England

RESTORING LOVE
©2001 by Debbie Alsdorf. All rights reserved.

Printed in the United States of America

1 2 3 4 5 6 7 8 9 10 Printing/Year 05 04 03 02 01

Unless otherwise noted, Scripture quotations are taken from the *Holy Bible: New International Version®*. Copyright © 1973, 1978, 1984 by International Bible Society. Used by permission of Zondervan Publishing House. All rights reserved. Additional Scripture taken from *The Amplified Bible Old Testament* (AMP), © 1962, 1964 by Zondervan Publishing House; *The Amplified Bible New Testament* (AMP), ©1954, 1958 The Lockman Foundation; *The Message* (TM) ©1993. Used by permission of NavPress Publishing House; The Holy Bible, *New Living Translation* (NLT), ©1996. Used by permission of Tyndale House Publishers, Inc., Wheaton, Illiois, 60189. All rights reserved. *King James Version* (KJV).

Editor: Afton Rorvik
Cover Design: Matthew C. DeCoste
Interior Design: Lisa A. Barnes

Library of Congress Cataloging-in-Publication Data

Alsdorf, Debbie.
    Restoring love / Debbie Alsdorf.
        p. cm.
    ISBN 0-7814-3383-5
        1. Love—Biblical teaching. 2. Interpersonal relations—Biblical teaching. 3. Christian women—Religious life. 4. Bible—Study and teaching. I. Title.

BS680.L64 A47 2000
241'.4—dc21   00-027251

Dedicated to
Sharon Leigh Montagna
God made us sisters, love has made us friends

&

Patti Prado
Who obeyed God and gave me three words:
"His Abiding Deliverance"

May God lead us all to the arms of the Deliverer and His Restoring Love—
a love that rebuilds and sets free those that are held in any type of captivity.

"He refreshes and restores my life—
He leads me in the paths of righteousness."
Psalm 23:3, AMP

Acknowledgments

God's restoring love rebuilds our lives, taking what has been broken and fashioning something new. I would like to thank the following people who have loved "broken me" along my path to restoration, as well as those who have helped with the ministry of this book.

Ed and Irene Kenzie—my mother and father, who now make their homes in heaven. Mom, how I thank you for opening up our past so we could move on into healing in your last years. I miss you. You are always in my heart and part of who I am. Daddy, it's been a long time since I have seen your face or heard your voice. Time doesn't change my love for you. I am thankful for God's restoration in your life, and I will always treasure the memory of your love for me.

Ray—my precious husband. You have walked through the valley with me. You have been an instrument of God's restoring love. Thanks. You are loved.

The girls in my family—my stepdaughters, Ashley and Megan, and my nieces, Denise, Cindy, Danille, and Corrie. Even though we are often far apart, you are always close to my heart. I pray God's love restores in each of us all the places that need His touch, building our lives into all that He has designed!

The women at Cornerstone Fellowship for allowing me to be "real" and "not perfect" in my place of ministry. I deeply desire to please God and serve Him. You women give me the courage to be real, bring me joy, and have been incredibly healing to my heart.

Beth Anne Moitoso—I'm grateful for your contagious joy!

Jan Tyler—your encouragment restores me!

Lori Sisemore—You are a Holy Spirit cheerleader!

Melanie Robbins—Melanie Robbins—I enjoy our times together; you ignite my passion for Christ. It's an honor to be called your "mentor."

Rene Biel—What a beautiful restored treasure you are. I love your heart.

Our Marriage Builders Group—past and present—You are all the best!

Bev Dixon—You are incredible, and I thank God for you and your walk with Him. It's been a pleasure serving with you.

Sue Boldt—Your light led me to new life in Christ in 1973. I will forever cherish you and be grateful for your faithfulness to God. It is because of you that I know my Deliverer and His love.

Pastors Steve Madsen, Bob Ferro, and Mark Calcagno—Thank you for everything. You have been an important part of my restoration in Christ.

My two little "baker boys" (not too little anymore!)—You are the best sons a mother could ever have asked for. Justin and Cameron . . . you are loved.

Lord Jesus—You have given me purpose and it is a wonderful thing to have a sense of direction in life. I can never thank You enough for Your faithfulness in my life, the life of my children, and in my heart of hearts. You truly are the restorer of my soul, my deliverer, and the God who never leaves me. Come, Lord Jesus!

CONTENTS

INTRODUCTION

Restoration is what the love of God is all about. *Restore* means to bring back to good health or vigor, to renew, to revive, to rebuild, and to refresh. Many of us women need the Master's restorative power to work in the broken places of our hearts and lives. We need to be brought back to our original, God-intended purpose of living and become women who bear fruit, walk in the Spirit, and live in the fullness of God's plan.

A woman living with purpose is a woman living with a determined goal or aim. She has focus. This focus for what she has deemed important fills her with a passion to carry out her goal and achieve her aim. The Apostle Paul had a determined purpose—to know Christ and to make Him known. He lived passionately despite circumstances that were sometimes too terrible to imagine. He was a person like us. If anything made him different, it would be the freedom and passion he displayed in his Christian walk.

Is freedom a reality in your life today? Do you put your hope in God's ability to deliver you, or do you remain stuck in the rut of hopelessness, a victim to every whim of circumstance? If I am to be totally real and honest, I must admit that many days I don't feel set free or delivered, and personal restoration often seems light-years away.

Some days I find myself wondering if anybody else still deals with negative junk in their lives, or if I am the only one who secretly struggles with bad habits, ugly thoughts, and ingrained negative patterns. Do others beat themselves up because their faith is waning, their relationships crumbling, and their attitude is "out to lunch"?

Are others secretly feeling bound to their image, strapped to perfection, and longing for approval? Is there anybody else who wishes she could rip off the church mask and be free to be herself . . . warts and all?

As insecurities mount, attitudes plummet, and broken hearts pave the way to broken lives. Locked up might sound more familiar than delivered or set free.

This is life, but is this freedom?

One thing for sure, we are all living out the pages of "real life." Some days I feel as if I am strolling joyfully down Main Street U.S.A. without a care in the world. Other times I feel as if I am stuck and lost on the Boulevard of Broken Dreams, struggling to make it through another day. Do the words *roller-coaster ride* mean anything to you?

The ups and downs of life are often hard to understand. It is easy to live out my Christian faith and principles when the sun is shining, but it's a challenge to keep living in faith and freedom when life is a torrent of rain.

Though not one person has a life free from troubles, there is good news: God is able to make all grace abound toward us, regardless of circumstances, so that we can be set free to live for Him. Living each day fully. Putting the past aside while trusting God's plan for our tomorrows.

I have personally experienced God's love as He has taken the broken pieces of my life and put me back together again. Strength that I could not find on my own I have found in Him.

In this study we will look at the amazing power of God to restore lives and also at the basic principles of living free. We will look at our negative patterns and childish behaviors, seeking to find new patterns in Christ. As we embrace the work of the cross and the wonderful grace of the Father, we will begin to realize the wonderful freedom that He has already provided for us.

This study is a devotional journey of the heart. Taking each lesson slowly is better than speed-reading it in one sitting. I encourage you to savor the Scriptures, ponder the meaning, and allow time for God to speak to you. Each lesson has approximately eleven to sixteen sections, which can be done over the course of a week. You may want to try doing two or three sections each day.

Begin each time of reading with prayer, asking God to make His Word alive and personal to you so that you can incorporate all that He has for you into your real, everyday life.

As you read the Bible, always keep the challenge of personal application in the forefront of your mind. The deepest, most profound truths are those we learn to apply to our "real" lives. His restoring love is powerful to set us free, imparting hope and passion for living.

On this I have set my hope: that He will continue to deliver me (2 Cor. 1:10).

Trusting in His restoring love,
Debbie Alsdorf

TIPS FOR GROUP MEMBERS

When working through this study in a group, the following suggestions may prove helpful.

- Have a purpose for your time together. What do you hope to accomplish in twelve weeks?
- Keep in step with the lesson, giving opportunity for personal sharing on the topic of each lesson and the message of each Scripture passage.
- Encourage one another to be real and provide a safe place for that.
- Keep all group conversation and sharing Christ-centered and confidential.
- Encourage practical application of each week's lesson, holding each other accountable.
- Pray before you begin, and pray when you end.

TIPS FOR GROUP LEADERS

It is a joy to see women open up and receive the restoring love of God for themselves. As God gives each woman personal clarity for her own life and walk with Him, you have the privilege of keeping her accountable and challenging her with the Word of Truth. The following suggestions may help you lead each woman in your group in her personal journey toward restoration.

∞ Make every effort to stay on track so that you study the Bible rather than just functioning as a social or support group. Though both social interaction and support are important, the main emphasis should first be the personal application and study of God's Word. (As you know, women can get off track!)

∞ Promote fellowship and unity within the group by accepting each woman right where she is today. Have a "No Stones" policy—women agree not to judge or throw stones at another woman who is struggling and seeking understanding within the group.

∞ Nurture each woman in her spiritual gifts, personal holiness, and in her interaction with the Word of God.

∞ Be real so others can be real too.

∞ Be honest as you work through the study so that others can feel safe confessing their faults and find healing as they learn to apply God's Word.

∞ Help women be accountable as they work through relationship issues.

∞ Pray for each woman in your group and take seriously the privilege of leading her in a study of God's Word.

Every day is a gift
to be opened
to be treasured
to be lived fully.

He Is Everything . . .

Understanding the Deliverer

Life. It is not as easy as we thought it would be. There are problems to solve, bills to pay, schedules to keep, and relationships to maintain. Real life happens when we wrestle with the alarm clock, pry open our eyes, and plant our two feet on the floor in the morning. From that point on anything goes. In real life we wrestle with things like crying babies, burned toast, flat tires, and lumpy gravy. We tango with teenagers, try to please people, suffer broken hearts, and spend our energies anywhere but in the Bahamas. No wonder we dream about Calgon taking us away! (For you younger gals . . . that means escaping in a tub of warm bath bubbles).

What do you wrestle with in your real life? Have you ever noticed that some problems just don't get solved? There are certain issues that have no solutions, and some circumstances that just keep repeating themselves. In this study we will look at Jesus as our deliverer from hopeless, purposeless living, and we will pay attention to how His power can reign in the middle of all our wrestling with "real" life issues.

It may come as a surprise to you, but Jesus would like you to know that He is everything you need in this life. He has the power to change your life from the inside out. Does that sound impractical to you? Well, maybe you just don't realize how close to you He actually is. Jesus doesn't live in a church building somewhere, anxiously awaiting the Sunday visitors. The Bible tells us that once we've believed in the Lord Jesus Christ and given our lives to Him, He lives within each one of us (John 14:20). He is always with us! Each day the Spirit of the living God resides in you. Have you ever stopped and thought about the Spirit of God living inside you?

"... I am in my Father, and you are in me, and I am in you" (John 14:20).

He is teaching you, guiding you, comforting you, and leading you along life's path.

Each of us has within us a void that only God can fill. Try as you might to fill it with other things—people, places, material possessions, drugs, alcohol, food, or the pursuit of pleasures—none of these things can continually fill or satisfy you. Once you fill up with them, you empty out just as quickly as you filled up. On empty again, you repeat the cycle. Frustration mounts until you finally say, "Here, God, take all of me and fill me with Yourself." Have you ever found yourself at this place?

He wants us to have the assurance that **He is everything** we need for the changing process that will draw us closer to Him and set us free for His purposes. He is in the business of restoring lives—rebuilding, reshaping, renewing, and reclaiming us for His purposes.

1. Let's look at the heart of Jesus. Read John 4:1-26.

In this passage we see Jesus interacting with a Samaritan woman. There were many cultural and religious reasons why Jesus should not have spoken to this woman.

First, she was a Samaritan, a hated mixed race that originated with the joining of the Jews and the foreigners that had been deported to Assyria (2 Kings 17:24). Jews considered Samaritans impure.

Second, she was known to be living in sin. Jewish religious leaders prided themselves in not associating with sinners.

Third, this was a public place where men would not normally interface with women. No respectable Jewish man would be seen speaking to this woman.

Jesus was never inhibited by man's rules or cultural standards. He was prepared to share the Good News with every person regardless of race, past sins, or social ranking. By all human reasoning of the day, the message for this woman should have been: "Three strikes and you're out, Samaritan woman!" Not so with Jesus; He had a message for her.

∞ To establish this life-changing message in your heart, write out John 4:10 and John 4:13-14.

∞ Living waters? What do you think Jesus meant by using those words?

Water is necessary for life and well-being. Water temporarily quenches the thirst and hydrates the body. Obviously, His living water is something different. It is water for the soul.

∞ Read Isaiah 55—an invitation to the thirsty. Underline or highlight verses in this chapter that are meaningful to you. Why were they meaningful to you?

∞ What is the outcome of what Jesus can give you?

Jesus gives completeness:
eternal life
intimate relationship with God now!
direction for living
fullness of joy and peace

2. Why did the Samaritan woman suspect Jesus was a prophet? (John 4:17-19)

∞ Write out Proverbs 5:21.

∞ Do you think you can keep things hidden from God? Explain.

Jesus was able to tell this woman things about herself and her past, not because He was a psychic or a fortuneteller, but because He is God. This same all-knowing, all-wise God knows everything about us. He knows our sins, yet He still extends relationship to us. He knows our small, puny faith, yet still offers us the best in our journey of life. He knows we get confused, distracted, and disillusioned, yet still calls us to Himself and to receive waters that don't run dry. He extends His hand to us and offers us *everything*.

3. What is John 4:23 saying to you?

∞ What kind of worshipers does the Father seek?

∞ Why must you worship God in spirit and in truth?

As Christians we can learn to say the right thing, do the right thing, and talk about the right thing, while not walking in the freedom (the *everything*) that He desires to give us. Church can become Christ with a building being the only sanctuary you are connected to. But regardless of the beauty of a building, it cannot be everything to you. It can't heal your heart or restore your life—it is just a building! The location of worship is not as important as the attitude of our hearts as we worship. And the sanctuary that God wants to teach us about is the very temple we live in each day: "Don't you know that you yourselves are God's temple and that God's Spirit lives in you?" (1 Cor. 3:16).

∞ What does John 4:24 say about God?

God is not like us physical beings. We are limited to one place at a time while He is present everywhere. Because of this He can be worshipped anytime and in any place. We try to put God in compartmental boxes, but He doesn't operate as we do.

◌ What did Jesus declare in John 4:26?

I am He! Who? He is the Messiah. The Samaritan woman knew the Messiah was coming, and now He declared that He was the Messiah. The Messiah was the expected ruler and deliverer of the Jewish people, whose coming was prophesied in the Old Testament. The main purpose of the Messiah was to *deliver*.

4. Read Isaiah 8:19-22 and 9:1-7.

◌ According to Isaiah 8, whom should you consult about life?

◌ What will describe you if you don't look to God?

◌ According to verse 22 what did the people see?

◌ Do you ever look at your life or the world around and see distress, darkness, and fearful gloom?

◌ Is it hard for you to grasp and believe the fact that despite the darkness, He is Everything? Why?

◌ God has given you a gift (Isa. 9:6). What or who is it?

◌ What will be on His shoulders?

This means that the authority for all things rests on His shoulders. This includes your life—past, present, and future. Let me repeat that: *this includes your life.*

∞ How does that truth help you today?

∞ What is He called? (Isa. 9:6)
1.
2.
3.
4.

Now list a few things you might be called today, if someone could see inside into the "real you." (e.g., angry, afraid . . .)

5. In light of your personal struggles that define the "real you" no one else may see, let's talk about His name, the power behind His name, and what that can mean for you as you walk with Him.

Wonderful Counselor

He is the one who gives the right advice.

Counselor comes from the Hebrew word *yaats*, which means to advise, resolve, guide, purpose. With those definitions I can say: "He is my wonderful advisor, my wonderful resolver, my wonderful guide, and my wonderful purpose!"

∞ Look up the definition of *wonderful* in a dictionary. Write it here.

Mighty God

He is God Himself.

Mighty comes from the Hebrew word *gibbor*, which means powerful, warrior, champion, chief, giant, strong. I can now say: "He is my powerful God, a warrior, and a champion. He is my giant God, and my strong God!"

∞ Look up *mighty* in a thesaurus. What did you find?

When I looked for other ways to describe *mighty* in a thesaurus, I found the word *strong*, which can also be defined as sound or sure. I like those descriptions.

My God is a sound God, a sure God, and He is my God! I also found that *mighty* can be described as vast, huge, or jumbo. Well, guess what? We have a God who is HUGE. The next time you are tempted to buckle under the temptation to fear or doubt, remember God is absolutely jumbo, huge, vast, and mighty!

Everlasting Father

He never changes. He is timeless. He is God our Father.

Everlasting comes from the Hebrew root *ad*, which means duration, continue, and advance. I can rejoice that He is a Father who will stay with me for the whole duration of the journey, continuing with me throughout my lifetime. He is a Father who gives me the advance, the next step.

∞ Check a thesaurus to find other ways to say *everlasting*. List some here.

One of the definitions I found for *everlasting* is "around the clock." He is my around-the-clock Father! He never sleeps. He cares for you and me nonstop! Some women have experienced rejection or abandonment. The pain of such an experience is real and is often carried around for years. We must all remember that it is never God who abandons. Though people can inflict real pain into our lives, God desires to set us free as we realize that He will always be with us 24/7!

Prince of Peace

He rules with justice and peace.

Prince is from the Hebrew *sar*, which means a head person, chief, captain, or keeper. Peace is from the Hebrew *shalom*, which means welfare, health, prosperity, and peace.

Wow! Now get this . . . I can call Him Prince of Peace, or in other words, I can say, "He is the keeper of my welfare!" Prince of peace means keeper of my welfare, my well-being. Need I say more? Now that is *everything I need* summed up in one single verse.

∞ Look up both *prince* and *peace* in a dictionary for an everyday application. Write down the definitions you find.

In my dictionary I found that a prince is a son of a sovereign and that a definition of peace is freedom. So Jesus, the Son of the Sovereign God, is my freedom!

6. **Throughout the Old Testament book of Isaiah we see the coming of the Messiah prophesied. This is valuable reading, as it helps us to recognize what He was coming to do, and how that relates to our personal lives today. Read Isaiah 11.**

∞ According to verses 2-3, what are all the adjectives explaining what Spirit would be in Jesus and upon Him?

∞ According to Isaiah 61:1-3, what are some of the things Christ is anointed to do?

∞ Jesus quoted these words of Isaiah in Luke 4:18-19. Read Luke 4:17-20 and write out Luke 4:18-19, the words of Christ.

Isaiah records the prophesy that God would rescue His people through a redeemer. Jesus is telling the people in Luke that He was the One they had heard about. That redeemer was Jesus! Now He had come to deliver God's people. *Deliverer* means in part to rescue, save, or set free. We see in these verses a loving God who is not only able to help His people, but also desires to rescue and deliver them.

∞ What are some of the personal applications you can find in Isaiah 61?

7. Read Psalm 18.

This is a psalm of deliverance. David sang this psalm to the Lord when the Lord rescued him from all his enemies and from Saul. (For more on that particular story read 2 Sam. 22:1-51).

∞ Write out Psalm 18:2.

This verse makes it clear that if we need protection we are to look to God, who is strong. David describes God's ability to deliver us from harm five ways.

1. God our rock. He cannot be moved, even by our enemy. Solid and secure are we with God as our rock.

2. God our fortress. He is a place of safety.

3. God our shield. He is a barrier that comes between us and everything that passes through our life. Some describe having this kind of a shield as having a "Father-filtered" life.

4. God the horn or strength of our salvation. Our salvation or deliverance doesn't rest on me. It rests on the strength of God; therefore, it is secure.

5. God is our stronghold. If we need help or protection, we are to look to God. He is the One who holds us with strength that cannot be measured, for He alone is mighty and powerful above all else. He created all things and by His will all things are held together. We can trust in Him and in His strong grip on our lives.

Once again we see that God is everything we need!

8. In Psalm 18, now concentrate on verses 16-19.

∞ Do your problems seem like deep waters? Explain.

∞ What does verse 16 say He will provide for you in the midst of deep waters?

When the deep waters of life threaten to drown you, remember that God is with you. In your situation He will either deliver you on the spot or be your support and strength as you walk through a life difficulty. In either case He will provide everything you need as you look to Him.

∞ With that in mind, write out Psalm 18:18.

∞ What was the Lord to David in his day of disaster?

The *King James Version* says, "the Lord was my stay." The *Amplified* version says, "but the Lord was my stay and my support." And, the *New Living Translation* says, "They attacked me at a moment when I was weakest, but the LORD upheld me."

It is clear that whether He chooses to take your present problem away right now or to allow you to walk through it for a season, He can and should be trusted with your situation. Your deep waters need to be given over to God as you call on the God who is everything you need.

9. Write out John 15:12.

Have you ever felt as if you had a powerful enemy, one that was too strong for you? Well . . . you do. And, this is a piece of information that is important for you to know and to remember throughout your walk with God.

We are to be alerted to the fact that we do have an enemy. 1 Peter 5:8

tells us: "Be self-controlled and alert. Your enemy the devil prowls around like a roaring lion looking for someone to devour." You can discount this as a myth, but we are also told: "All Scripture is God-breathed and is useful for teaching, rebuking, correcting and training in righteousness, so that the man of God may be thoroughly equipped for every good work" (2 Tim. 3:16).

He delivered me from my strong enemy, and from them which hated me: for they were too strong for me (Ps. 18:17, KJV).

Part of being equipped for every good work is being informed. The fact is: we have an enemy. But God does not leave us hanging in midair with an enemy tearing us to shreds. NO! He tells us He is everything we need—He is our deliverer from the hands of the enemy.

∞ Write out James 4:7-8.

∞ According to 1 John 3:8, what did the Son of God come to do?

10. Read Hebrews 2:14-18.

∞ What is this saying to you, regarding God's ability to deliver you and be everything you need?

11. Read Hebrews 1:1-3.

Jesus sustains all things by His powerful word! This is not just some poetic statement; it is a fact. He sustains you, He holds you, He counsels you, and He is mighty on your behalf. He protects you, He delivers you, He rescues you, He gives you peace, and He brings you joy. He turns your mourning into dancing, and He surrounds you with His love. What more do I need to point out?

Can you conclude with me that *He is everything you need?*

12. Write out Exodus 3:14.

God's most powerful description of Himself is recorded here when He says, "I AM." He is everything that is perfect, excellent, and flawless. He was from the beginning and will be until the end. He is it!

EVERYTHING . . . you will ever need Him to be to fulfill yourself.

EVERYTHING . . . you will ever need to be conformed into His image.

EVERYTHING . . . you will ever need to have confidence.

EVERYTHING . . . you will ever need to experience peace.

EVERYTHING . . . you will ever need to live productively in this life.

13. Write down your thoughts on this "everything" concept (truth).
∞ Write out 2 Peter 1:3.

14. Read Hebrews 3:1.

∞ On what are you to fix your thoughts?

God has given us Jesus Christ. He came to rescue us from the bondage of sin and death. He came to be our deliverer. He is our salvation. God has given us everything we need in Jesus. You might be going through hard times, but remember—there is a God in heaven. And this God in heaven is your deliverer. He is everything you need!

As recorded in the Book of Daniel (Dan. 2:25-28), when called upon to interpret a dream, Daniel told the king that no wise man, enchanter, magician, or diviner could explain the mystery in the dream. But Daniel did say, "There is a God in heaven, **who can reveal** mysteries."

Today, I encourage you to remember that there is a God in heaven. We want answers now! We want solutions to our problems and provisions for our needs this minute. We often look to other people and to other things to supply an answer, solution, or comfort. Today go straight to the source—the Mighty God in heaven who is the keeper of your welfare, the Prince of Peace, and your Jumbo God. He can handle everything that concerns you, and He alone has the answers to the mysteries of life.

This week I encourage you to tell yourself this truth over and over: **There is a God in heaven and He is everything I need (Dan. 2:28, 2 Peter 1:3).**

As we grow to know God more personally and intimately, we will grow in freedom. As we travel down the journey to freedom, let us always hold fast to the truth of who our Deliverer is. He promises to continue to deliver us and in that we can find hope.

"On Him we have set our hope that He will continue to deliver us" (2 Cor. 1:10).

Dear Lord,

I come to You with a grateful heart. You are everything! This is hard to fully comprehend, but I ask You to enable me to get an understanding of this truth. When life surrounds me with its routines, dilemmas, and questions, I ask You to be my stay. I want to fix my eyes on You. I want You to be my focus. Then in the midst of deep waters, I will not drown, for You will be my help. You will be my guide and You will be my counselor. Lord, give me Your hand today that I might be pulled to strength, hope, health, and peace. Amen.

So, my dear Christian friends, companions in following this call to the heights, take a good hard look at Jesus. He's the centerpiece of everything we believe, faithful in everything God gave him to do (Heb. 3:1, TM).

Everything that goes into a life of pleasing God has been miraculously given to us by getting to know, personally and intimately, the One who invited us to God (2 Peter 1:3, TM).

HE REDEEMS ME

Uncovering the Beauty of the Lost and Found

What a find! I thought as I quickly snatched up the rickety-looking chair from the pile of junk at a garage sale. It was just what I was looking for. To anyone else it probably looked like just an old, worn-out chair that was layered with several coats of paint. Practically three-legged, it wobbled when I touched it. But despite its obvious flaws, I knew this chair was going to be beautiful once I worked my crafter's magic on it.

Beneath the layered paint was a beautiful grain of oak. Why would anybody want to cover it up with gloppy old paint? Slowly and steadily, as I worked on it, the chair began to take on a new identity. What had been just an obvious piece of junk was now becoming a beautiful little side chair, soon to take center stage in a room filled with country furnishings. Once it was finished I was amazed at how beautiful, functional, and special this chair had become to me.

Just like this little chair, worn-out and broken from use, we too need someone to recover us from the heap of life's pieces and make us new. Our carefully applied paint is chipping and showing signs of distress. Our legs that keep us upright and functioning will need some extra strength glue to carry us through the journey.

We need to be pulled out of the trash heap and reclaimed for the beautiful, functional, and special woman God has designed us to be.

Now, there's good news and bad news . . . which would you like first?

Well, the bad news is: we are all worn down by the stress and pressures of real life. Some of us are actually "missing in action." We are so actively charting our own course that we have no idea what "spot" we were originally created for. We are lost. We've lost touch with ourselves and our Maker.

But the good news is: Jesus Christ came to recover us from the bad news of broken-down, empty, and directionless living. He has redeemed us. That means He bought us back, recovered us, and purchased our freedom.

He purchased us! Like that little broken-down chair . . . once I purchased it, it was mine. I knew the plans I had for it. Plans to strip it, sand it, and make it not only functional, but also beautiful again.

I had good plans for this chair; after all, I bought it, didn't I? I had a future spot for it in a sunny little corner, and in my mind I knew exactly how I would adorn it with a floral pillow. I could see this all long before the work was complete. Once finished, I knew I would joyfully display my creative work. It would be an example of what I could do with an old junky chair, a little time, a little work, and lots of love.

> *"For I know the plans I have for you," declares the* LORD, *"plans to prosper you and not harm you, plans to give you hope and a future" (Jer. 29:11).*

God purchased you, so now you are His. He knows the plans He has for you. He bought you, didn't He? He will take the broken-down pieces of your life, and with a little time, the Holy Spirit's work, and lots of love, He will make you strong and functional. He has redeemed you . . . and me.

1. Read Exodus 6:1-9.

The people of Israel were in bondage in Egypt. The book of Exodus is about their departure or exit from Egypt and all the miracles that God performed to deliver them. Moses was the key player here in the plan of God. In his own strength Moses was weak and unsure, but God made him strong in order to accomplish His will.

> *For all have sinned and fall short of the glory of God, and are justified freely by His grace through the redemption that came by Christ Jesus (Rom. 3:23–24).*

∞ How did God promise to redeem the children of Israel from the Egyptians?

Note that He says, "I will redeem you. . . . I will take you as my own people" (Exodus 6:6-7). But even though He made a promise of deliverance from bondage, the people did not take it seriously. They didn't listen—no pat answers for them—because they had been the victims of cruel bondage and discouragement! Perhaps you haven't listened either. Has God been reaching out to redeem you with an outstretched arm, but you are so discouraged that you just turn your head and walk the other way?

As Christian women, God is talking to us. Have we forgotten Him? Do we neglect to live in the power of the redemption He has already provided for us? Christ has redeemed us by His blood on the cross, and now He has the power of redeeming us . . . each day making more of our hearts and minds His.

> Very rarely will anyone die for a righteous man, though for a good man someone might possibly dare to die. But God demonstrates His own love for us in this: While we were still sinners, Christ died for us (Rom. 5:7-8).

You are His. (I know this is a repeat so listen up.) He found you, pulling you out of a life in which you could not see or understand spiritual things. He is now working in you, redeeming every area of your life. He takes the paint off, layer by layer. He strips and sands off your rough, jagged edges. He purchased you with the price of His blood—this is redemption.

2. Read Psalm 49.

∞ What does this psalm say in verses 7-8 regarding redeeming a life?

Most people express a strong desire for more freedom in their life. God in His Word lets us know that such a freedom is possible. Jesus promised, "You will know the truth, and the truth will set you free" (John 8:32). Still, very few are experiencing freedom. We often go through our entire lives looking for truth and understanding within. Are we missing the truth in our life? Jesus is the truth! (John 14:6) Is knowing Jesus our main goal?

When Christ recovers us, pulling us out of the pile, buying us back, paying the price—redeeming us—He is offering the freedom and truth we so long for.

How often have we looked to others to redeem us and make us happy? We look to people for approval and happiness. We look to people for meaning and purpose, and we look to people for freedom from our inner turmoil. When we don't or can't get what we need, we just get the brush out and slap on another layer of paint! We cover up the ugly stuff that God is so capable of redeeming. We need to quit looking to people. No one can redeem us. We need to quit looking to things. Nothing will go to the grave with us. But in life and death, God is always with us, and He always redeems us with His outstretched hand.

∞ Write out Matthew 16:26.

You can gain popularity, prestige, financial security, and every earthly benefit, but you can't take any of it with you. No amount of money, manipulation, program, or advantages can save your soul. You could never be rich enough to buy your soul and pay the price. So, Jesus did it for you . . . and me. Now, we need to learn what it means to live as one who is redeemed (or recovered and rescued from the trash heap).

3. Read Ephesians 2:1-3.

∞ How many years did you live dead in your sins?

∞ What does this passage say you followed during that time?

∞ Do you think you developed as a person during those years?

∞ Do you suppose you developed patterns of thought and actions during those years? Explain.

As negative as the description of us in this Ephesians verse sounds, we cannot overlook what it is saying. We are quick to grasp the positive verses that offer blessing and love, but we look the other way when faced with the truth in the verses that outline to us our condition apart from Christ. It is vitally important that we understand we are sinners. This is the bottom line: we are sinners, we need a Savior, and we need our Redeemer—Jesus.

> Many of the patterns that were developed by the flesh when we were young may be responsible for most of our struggles today.[1]—*Robert McGee*

So What Is Freedom?

Freedom is escaping the grasp of anything that desires to capture and enslave us. Freedom is breaking loose from the chains that bind us emotionally and mentally. Freedom is breaking away from habits that threaten to destroy the good things that God has for us, such as health, security, and peace.

Before we can experience freedom, we must recognize our need for a deliverer and our need to depend on God's restoring love. Though it is not popular to speak of our sinful nature, or the depravity of humankind, it is a subject that deserves honest reflection for the Christian woman. In order to depend on a deliverer, we must recognize the condition of our human flesh. We must humble ourselves before Almighty God if we are to begin to trust in Him completely.

4. Write out Ephesians 4:18.

∞ What does it mean to have a darkened understanding?

When our minds develop apart from God, we will have a darkened understanding of life. For most of us our minds were developed while in the darkroom of the world we live in and in the dysfunction of the family units we were raised in. I like to think that God takes the "dys" out of the dysfunction and makes our lives functional when He redeems us, showing us how to walk in the freedom of His grace and restoring love.

5. Read Hebrews 10:22.

∞ What kind of conscience does this verse say you have?

∞ Write out Genesis 6:5.

∞ What are the natural thoughts and inclinations of the human heart?

6. Read Jeremiah 17:9.

∞ What is the main thought of this verse?

∞ What does a heart beyond cure mean to you?

> When our thoughts are distorted, our emotions reflect the quality of those thoughts. Many times our hearts are deceitful because they are first deceived. But because of our darkened understanding, we don't realize our hearts are deceived. If I asked you to list ten things you are deceived about, you couldn't do it. The very nature of being deceived is that the deception goes unnoticed.[2]—*Robert McGee*

We have sick hearts! This indicates abnormality and not functioning according to God's original design and plan. Our hearts have been poisoned with fleshly, human, destructive input since the day we were born. Jeremiah ends the thought with, "who can understand it?" No one can understand the human heart, except for the Maker of our heart. When we try to fix ourselves and deliver ourselves with human wisdom, we become bound—instead of freed.

∞ Write out Romans 8:7.

If my mind is hostile to God, I will not be inclined to do things God's way. When I live my life according to my way, it is no surprise that I continue to struggle.

7. Read Galatians 1:1-5.

∞ What is this passage saying to you?

∞ Write out Galatians 1:4.

∞ For what did Christ give Himself over?

This present evil age is dark. Jesus came to be our salvation in the midst of a dark and daily decaying world.

Rescue: *extricate from an undesirable state; reclaim, salvage, deliver, salvation*

∞ What in your life do you need reclaimed today?

It is the will of God to rescue you. Will you take hold of the life preserver and depend on His strength for living, or will you continually submit yourself to daily drowning, rather than daily rescue?

⬯ Read Galatians 2:20. What is this saying to you about your life?

The laying down of your life enables you to reach for the lifesaver. Your life then becomes about the One who saved it, and not about you.

8. Read Galatians 3:1-14.

⬯ According to Scripture are you redeemed because you just decided to be redeemed, followed a program, joined a church, or adhered to rules that gave you the appearance of "getting it together"? Explain.

⬯ Have you ever been guilty of forgetting the redemption and grace you have received from the Lord? Elaborate.

⬯ What do you think is meant by the phrase, *begun in the Spirit*?

The Apostle Paul calls his readers foolish Galatians, and asks, "Who has bewitched you?" (3:1) This word *bewitched* comes from the Greek word, *baskaino*, which means to fascinate by false representation or to malign. Our culture is fascinated by a false representation of what is right and wrong. As Christian women we can be just as fascinated by a false representation of works and perfection. We can get just as caught up in the "I'll do it all by myself" mentality as anyone. But it is foolish! Why are we trying to be good instead of just trusting ourselves to the only ONE who is good? When we focus on redeeming ourselves and making ourselves better people, we no longer focus on God. It becomes all about "us," and that is not redemption. Instead, we should be reading the Word of God, learning more about who He is, and discovering daily what His design for life is. We should be coming to Him daily in relationship and fellowship, letting our relationship with Him change us from the inside out.

Listen, you have a Redeemer. You can not redeem yourself. It has already been done for you. I pray that your heart will experience hope and peace as you put the truth in your mind.

Even Job, while in the middle of terrible things said: "I know that my Redeemer lives, and that in the end he will stand upon the earth" (Job 19:25).

Redeemer comes from the Hebrew *gaal*, meaning to be the next of kin, to buy back and make relative, deliverer, purchase, ransom, revenger. You have a redeemer, someone who paid the price to make you His own.

* Thank God right now for providing a Redeemer for you. Thank Him that you are His. Praise Him this moment for all that this means in your everyday life. Ask God through His Holy Spirit to show you how real He can be in your everyday life and experience.

9. Focus now on Galatians 3:6-14. What is this passage saying to you?

∞ Write out Galatians 3:14.

∞ Why did He redeem you?

The promise of the Spirit means that the Spirit of God will dwell in me, teach me, instruct me, guide me, comfort me, pray for me, fill me, and anoint me for God's purposes.

10. Write out the following verses.
• John 14:16-17

• 2 Corinthians 1:21-22

• 2 Corinthians 3:17

• 2 Corinthians 5:5

> Satan has opposed the doctrine of the Spirit filled life about as bitterly as any other doctrine there is. He has confused it, opposed it, surrounded it with false notions and fears. He has blocked every effort of the Church of Christ to **receive from the Father her divine and blood-bought patrimony.** The Church has tragically neglected this great liberating truth—that there is now for the child of God a full and wonderful and completely satisfying anointing with the Holy Ghost.
>
> The Spirit filled life is not a special, deluxe edition of Christianity. It is a part and parcel of the total plan of God for His people. There is nothing about the Holy Spirit queer or strange or eerie. . . . The Holy Spirit is the Spirit of Jesus, and is as gracious and beautiful as the Savior Himself.[3] —*A. W. Tozer*

∞ What was the most meaningful part of these Scripture verses for you? I noticed that I have "Hooray!!!" written in the margin of my Bible, next to John 14:17: "He lives with you and will be in you." Does anything jump out at you and make you want to say "Hooray!!"?

11. Read 1 Peter 1:18-21.

∞ What is this saying to you?

Is your faith and hope in God today? Or is there a little "Pandora's box" that you have held away from God, saying in your heart: "God, I give you everything except_____." Since we have a Redeemer, a Deliverer, and a God who is closer than any kin, we can have peace and put our hope and faith in Him alone. It's like putting all the eggs in one basket—the basket of Jesus Christ, our Redeemer who lives!

12. Write out the following verses.
 • Ephesians 1:7-8

 • Colossians 1:13-14

13. Read Jeremiah 31:10-14.

∞ From what is the Lord redeeming His people? (v. 11)

∞ What will the redeemed be like?

∞ What will be gone from them, and what will replace it?

    I almost want to leap for joy as I read the words in this Jeremiah passage. What often seems stronger than me is life itself. The yoke and burden at different times and seasons seem too hard to carry. But my God redeems me from all that is too strong for me. He satisfies me with Himself and the abundance of His Spirit. I then grow and thrive like a well-watered garden. My leaf does not become brown and withered; instead it remains healthy and green because it is continually nourished by the water only God can give. In this I have much in common with the Samaritan woman who learned of living waters!

    I once was a lost woman. Growing up in an environment that was not immersed in the truth of God, I picked up all kinds of things over the years that bound me in chains. But Jesus found me. He drew me to Himself, put His light in my life, and His Spirit within me. I was missing in action . . . actively trying to live the best life that I could. I tried to do my best, but I could not save myself. Jesus took the lost girl and saved her from a life that was too big for her. As I worked on my little chair, He is working on me, making me beautiful and useable. In the same way He works on you too.

Our Redeemer lives! Don't allow yourself to forget it.

And because He lives, I can trust that He is always working. Just like me and my little chair—what once started out as a broken chair in a heap of junk became a treasured possession of mine. Sure, it took a lot of work. But the work didn't make it mine, the purchase did. The work only proved how much I wanted that chair. The work showed I could see beauty underneath those ugly layers. The work showed I had a plan and a place for my little treasure and proved that I wanted it.

You are God's little treasure! You might think you are hiding safely behind layers of paint. Honestly the regular eye will see only the new, fresh color you are painted today. But God sees beneath the layers to the very heart of you. He isn't impressed by the paint. In fact, He knows that sometimes it's the paint that keeps us from trusting Him! We become afraid to be real, afraid for anyone to know who we really are underneath it all. We don't have to be afraid any longer. God knows the plans He has for each of us. He knows how He desires to redeem us and draw us daily close to Himself. He has only our best interest in mind, because He created us for His purposes. We are His treasure!

∞ What was the most meaningful part of this lesson for you?

Dear Lord,

Thank You for paying the price for me. Your purchase on the cross makes the awesome power of Your spirit available to me. Strip the layers, get to the heart of me. Refinish me, renew me, transform my life by Your work on my behalf. Now I can be alive in You, and You in me. Your Spirit will always be with me. You will always uphold me. May I never forget the human condition and my need for You. Thank You for paying the price. Somehow thank-You doesn't seem enough . . . but it is a start. Amen.

For you are a people holy to the LORD your God. The LORD your God has chosen you out of all the peoples on the face of the earth to be His people, His treasured possession (Deut. 7:6).

HE SETS ME FREE

Moving away from Destructive Patterns and Childish Behaviors

Imagine that you are an ice skater in competition. You are in first place with one more round to go. If you perform well, the trophy is yours. You are nervous, anxious, and frightened. Then only minutes before your performance, your trainer rushes to you with the thrilling news: "You've already won! The judges tabulated the scores, and the person in second place can't catch you. You are too far ahead." Upon hearing that news, how will you feel? Exhilarated!

And how will you skate? Timidly? Cautiously? Of course not. How about courageously and confidently? You bet you will. You will do your best because the prize is yours. You will skate like a champion because that is what you are! You will hear the applause of victory. . . . The point is clear: the truth will triumph. The father of truth will win, and the followers of truth will be saved.[1]—*Max Lucado*

According to the *Oxford American Dictionary, free* means:
- Not fixed or held down
- Able to move without hindrance
- To be set at liberty (no longer in confinement)

Many people today are held down and held back in life because they are hindered by insecurities, fears, hang-ups, negative patterns, isolation, and various types of bondage. Christian women are just as prone to these hindrances too. Why? Because Christians are people, and people have problems. And people need the Lord.

Often in our hurry to fix things and overspiritualize our problems, we Christians skate right past the most important thing that we need to do—getting on our face before Almighty God. We need to humble ourselves before God and quit thinking and acting as if we have it all together. You can fool some people, but you can't fool God. He knows you inside out. And even with that incredible knowledge of you, He loves you. And it's because He loves you that He desires to set you free from the things that hold you down and restrict you from experiencing the fullness of His design for your life. Some of the things that hold me down are the childish things that I continue to act out and do, even in my adult life.

Humbling myself before Him means acknowledging the fact that I do not have it together and that I need the help and power of my Savior. There is only one way to be free, and that is through Jesus Christ.

1. Read John 8:31-36.

∞ Write out the following verses.
• John 8:32

• John 8:36

The Jews' response to Jesus was to say they had never been slaves and didn't see the need to be set free. Does this describe you at times? Many of us live in denial. We think if it isn't broken, why fix it? But far too often, it *is* broken and needs to be fixed and made whole.

> Common sense should tell us that the coping mechanisms we develop as small children will not continue to be effective as adults. Physical and spiritual maturity should be accompanied by a change in the way we handle problems and behave under stress. Too often, however, this is not the case.[2]—*Robert McGee*

2. Write out John 14:6.

∾ What three things does Jesus claim to be in John 14:6?

Part of our problem comes when we neglect to recognize the fact that in Jesus Christ we can find all of the answers we need for living. We fall easily into a trap that leads us to reason that not all of God's Word is relevant to our lives today. But the truth is that every word of God and every principle in Scripture is not only relevant, but it also frees us from bondage. Remember: the truth will free you—Jesus is the truth.

And just what is bondage? It is slavery! A slave is someone who is dominated by another or another's influence. Do you want to live in bondage or slavery? God has more for you than being a slave to the patterns of this world, the messages of your past, or the expectations of your social circle. God even has more for you than being a slave to significance and value through ministry and service. The only one you should ever be sold out to is Jesus Christ!

Christians and non-Christians alike are being held captive and are living in bondage to the schemes of the Devil and the desires of the flesh nature. Christians are being held captive by the lies of the Enemy **because they don't know the truth.**

We live in an age, when once saved, Christians want to water down the message, making it more palatable. We want a blessing, but we don't want to be asked to sacrifice anything. We want our prayers answered, but we don't want the responsibility that might go with the answered prayers. We want a quick fix to our problems and a better self to express to the world around us. In other words, we have become self-seeking Christians, living to please ourselves and others rather than living to please God. **This is bondage.** We have become locked up within ourselves, and we don't know how to become free.

In *Search for Freedom*, Robert McGee speaks of the process that has locked us up.

Stage 1—We are born and know little if anything about truth.

Stage 2—As we're growing up, people around us teach us what life is all about:
Who we are.
Whom to trust.
What's good or bad.
What we are worth.
What life and this world are all about.

Stage 3—The things we are told become a system of beliefs upon which we evaluate all new incoming information, accepting or rejecting as we compare it with our basic beliefs.

Stage 4—Our definition of truth becomes whatever it is that we have been taught, and our beliefs begin to dictate our behavior.

Maybe you grew up with some faulty life skills. Some of us were not raised in Christian homes. Some of us were raised in homes where Christ was believed in, but not lived in. We have picked up faulty thinking. This isn't psychology 101; it is just a life fact for most of us. My father was an alcoholic, and my mother was emotionally distant. We did not talk about problems. We lived as if nothing was wrong. My mother worked hard and wasn't home much while my father slipped up over and over, often being the cause of disruptive fights and silent storms in our home. I was basically alone, trying to figure out myself and life. Naturally, in my own immaturity I developed some terrible coping skills and some definite misbeliefs about myself and life.

At the age of 17, I came to know Jesus Christ. I was excited about this newfound relationship. I read my Bible all the time, attended many church services, and changed my circle of friends and social behaviors. But, what I never sought to change were my well-ingrained, unhealthy thought patterns.

Not that I could change them within my own puny effort anyway, but I never even acknowledged that they needed to change! I prayed and received deliverance for the "biggies," such as my teenage drinking style, but I never realized that my heart attitudes, thought processes, and habitual behaviors that were negative and unhealthy were just as big and may prove to be bigger later in life. Jesus Christ wants to set us free—truly free, in all areas, big and small.

3. Read 1 Corinthians 13:11-13.

∞ What did the Apostle Paul put behind him?

∞ The following is a list of some childish ways that you might have picked up along the way as unhealthy and unproductive patterns. Circle those that apply to you.

Blaming	Temper tantrums	Clinging	Crying
Lying	Bickering	Talking too much	Whining
Not listening	Exaggerating	Seeking approval	Interrupting
Arguing	Strong-willed	Tattling	Overeating
Underrating	Minimizing	Living in denial	Envy
Self-destructiveness	Self-hatred	Hopelessness	Fear
Causing chaos	Withdrawal	Pouting	Suspicious
Disrespectful	Gossiping	Undecided	Ashamed
Insecure	Helpless	Hostile	Rage
Negative	Aggressive	Insignificant	Jealous
Inferior	Inadequate	Irritated	Skeptical
Perfection	Performance	Pleasing	Beauty addict

Now, as we continue through this lesson, keep in mind that your areas of childish weakness are no surprise to Jesus. He alone can give you the power to put behind you things that are not healthy and are actually hindering your growth as a woman in Him. We are not to get introspective to the point of losing spiritual focus, but we must look honestly at our lives in the light of Jesus. Being set free does not require introspection but it does require awareness. We are not after self-help or self-improvement, but instead we are after walking and living in the Spirit of the living God—freedom.

> We must be aware of what our own danger conditions are. We must become aware of our personal tendencies if we are to learn how to be good watchmen. Warning: we easily run from the need of self-examination. We know that the Bible teaches that we should make a habit of checking to see if our actions line up with God's will, but many of us are afraid of self-examination. Therefore, we don't do it. We need to admit our resistance, acknowledge that it is necessary if we are going to ask God to set us free from nagging flesh behaviors and become first class watchmen. Even though we still have the desire to sin, or do things our way—we now, as Christians have the power to run to God.[3]

4. Read Galatians 5.

∞ What would a broad-stroke overview of this chapter look like?

∞ Let's sift through the message in Galatians 5. In verse 1, what is the reason that Christ set you free?

Again—what is freedom?
- Did not want us to be fixed or held down by the world.
- Wanted to set us at liberty to love and serve only Him.
- Wanted to enable us to live unrestricted lives so that we might live, breathe, and move in the Spirit's power.

∞ What are you told not to let happen again?

The early Christians were legalistic in approach. It wasn't uncommon for them to fall back into trusting in the laws and religious regulations of the day. When living to keep only the rules, we become like slaves. Our relationship with the Father gets reduced to something God didn't intend it to be. We were created to have intimacy with the Father. In order for this to be so, we must not rely on rules, people, things, or other methods of attaining approval, significance, or righteousness. To be free we must stay focused on Christ and His work on the cross. Jesus is the one who removed the yoke of bondage. Don't go back to it! Don't settle. God has more for you than bondage, rule-keeping, and the torment that comes from trying to live up to a standard that can never be fully attained.

Christ set us free so we can live for Him, not so others can think we are better people or that we have it together. To live for Christ is to live unselfishly. When we go back to our own selfish desires, we are running back to the shackles of bondage. We are saying, "Quick, get the key and lock me up!" On the contrary, when we purpose in our hearts to live a life of surrender and trust, we are saying, "Thank You, dear God, for unlocking me and releasing me from the torment of living only for selfish desires."

5. Let's look over verses 2-4.

Circumcision was a symbol of doing the right thing. It symbolized the right background and absolute adherence to religious rules. It was a way to find favor with God. But when Christ came, He came to deliver us from the bondage that rules and regulations represented. Instead of rules, He showed us a way to relationship and responsibility.

∞ Why did Paul say that if you were circumcised, you were obligated to all of the law?

∞ What does that mean to you today?

∞ Are you trusting in anything other than the cross of Christ for salvation and freedom to live? Explain.

∞ What does Paul say happens to you when you try to justify yourself by anything other than the blood of Christ?

Alienated: *unfriendly or hostile*	∞ Do you want this to describe your relationship with God? Elaborate.

We need to be set free from trying to "do life" our way. When living in our power, we are hostile towards God, alienated from Him and His glorious plan for us. We've exchanged freedom for slavery. Yuck!

6. In Galatians 5:4 what does that statement "fallen away from grace" mean to you?

Grace is God's love in action. It is an undeserved and freely given gift. It is His power in you, doing in and through you that which you could never accomplish yourself. It is the manifestation of His restoring love actively working in you, though you don't deserve it. It is unmerited, undeserved favor. It is the essence of the Gospel, the message of salvation, and the pathway to living a life of freedom.

∞ According to Galatians 5:6, what has value and what does not?

∞ According to Galatians 5:7-10, what in your life causes you to trust yourself instead of God?

7. Write out Galatians 5:13.

∞ To what were you called?

∞ Whom are you to serve and by what method?

∞ What does Galatians 5:14-15 say about how you should live as a free woman?

It takes a freed woman to walk in the love of God toward others. It is often humiliating and a flesh burner to love those who do not love us back or those who don't like us. Our lifestyle should not be based on another's behavior—good or bad. Don't give someone that power over you. That is bondage at its best. What happens when we don't walk in the freedom of loving others? What is a sign or symptom that we are in bondage again? These symptoms cause a certain consequence to take place—what is it?

8. In Galatians 5:16 Paul tells you to live differently. What does Galatians 5:16-18 tell you about how you should live?

I find it interesting that God's remedy to living in bondage to the flesh is not trying harder to get our act together, but instead, seeking more intimacy with the Father and walking more closely in the Spirit. Remember, our flesh and spirit are in conflict with one another.

9. In Galatians 5:19-21, what are some of the acts of our sinful nature that we can be held captive to, or live in bondage to?

∽ What do you struggle with that is on this list?

∽ Who will not inherit the kingdom of God?

∽ Do these verses say, "those who are tempted or struggle with such things," or "those that willfully live in the flesh?"

10. What is the fruit of the Spirit?

∽ How does the fruit of the Spirit compare with the things you circled as some childish patterns in which you might still be living?

∽ What does Galatians 5:24 say about how you are to live? What does it mean to crucify something?

∽ Look up *crucify* in a dictionary. Record the definition here.

∽ Write out Galatians 5:25. *Memorize this verse.*

∽ Are you in step with the Spirit? Why or why not?

∞ What does Galatians 5:26 tell you not to do?

∞ Do you have a habit of envying other women or what they have? Explain.

∞ Is this practice of envy keeping you in bondage, or is it living in step with the Spirit?

Competition for young girls starts as early as the playground in kindergarten. Who is the best? Who is the prettiest? Whom do the little boys like? Who has the most friends? Who has the best clothes? Time to grow up, don't you think?

11. Read Galatians 6.

∞ What is the main theme or message of this chapter?

∞ How can you deceive yourself?

∞ Look up the definition of *compare* and write it here.

∞ Is it wrong to compare yourself with another woman? Explain.

∞ How has this affected you in the past?

∞ Do you struggle with this behavior today? How?

12. Write out Psalm 139:23-24.

∞ Is it OK to examine and scrutinize your own life and your personal behaviors? Why?

> *But let every person carefully scrutinize and examine and test his own conduct and his own work. He can then have the personal satis-faction and joy of doing something commendable [in itself alone] without [resorting to] boastful comparison with his neighbor (Gal. 6:4, AMP).*

Sometimes Christians are afraid to look inside. I don't know what we fear because God already sees the whole thing. It is biblical to look at a behavior that is not God's best for us and ask Him to work in us so that our behaviors might begin to line up with His Word and the walk of the Spirit.

13.   Write out Galatians 6:7-8.

∞   How do you benefit by living in bondage to your flesh?

∞ What do you gain by living in the freedom of God's Spirit?

14. What does Paul say is the only thing that counts, according to Galatians 6:15?

You are a new creation, created in Christ Jesus to live in freedom. You were made new by the Spirit of Christ. You have the mind of Christ. You were not born with the mind of Christ, but you have it now. In the past you operated with a child's mind that was shaped by the world you lived in. Now, you have resurrection power living in you, maturing you in all things. You have the truth living in you. You are a temple of God's Spirit. You are free to walk in love. You are free to make Spirit-led choices that will produce godly changes. Why on earth would you want to go back to living as if you never knew Christ or were never touched by His Spirit? You need to stand firm, don't you?

∞ Journal your thoughts on what you have read in the Book of Galatians and how it relates to you growing up in Christ and being set free from destructive or childish patterns.

It is absolutely clear that God has called you to a free life. Just make sure that you don't use this freedom as an excuse to do whatever you want to do and destroy your freedom. Rather, use your freedom to serve one another in love; that's how freedom grows. For everything we know about God's Word is summed up in a single sentence: Love others as you love yourself. That's an act of true freedom. If you bite and ravage each other, watch out—in no time at all you will be annihilating each other, and where will your precious freedom be then?

My counsel is this: Live freely, animated and motivated by God's Spirit. Then you won't feed the compulsions of selfishness. For there is a root of sinful self-interest in us that is at odds with a free spirit, just as the free spirit is incompatible with selfishness. These two ways of life are antithetical, so that you cannot live at times one way and at times another way according to how you feel on any given day. Why don't you choose to be led by the Spirit and so escape the erratic compulsions of a law-dominated existence? (Gal. 5:13-18, TM).

Dear Lord,

Forgive me for the times that I try to live on my own strength. I want to rely on You and the freedom that You give. I don't want to revert to my old way of life, living to please only myself. I want to live to please You, honor You, and move in step with Your Spirit. Thank You, Jesus, that You came to unlock the areas of my life that have held me in bondage. You are the One who can take negative patterns and turn my mind to positive biblical truth. Jesus, I ask You to mature me and grow me up. May I put aside childish things by the power of Your Spirit working in me and by this same Spirit may I grow more intimately close to You. Amen.

HE DEFINES ME

Discovering a New Identity in Him

All of us grew up with messages from our past. As we were developing, the messages ingrained within us were developing too. Once developed, they portrayed a picture of what we thought about life, ourselves, and God.

I grew up in the wave of the women's liberation movement. When I was a little girl, women in America were changing and so were their roles. Woman wanted to stand up and be noticed and did so by rallies, protests, and a flurry of new attitudes that infiltrated the women in our country. I was growing up in a time when women were redefining who they were and what they stood for.

Now I understand the impact of what was accomplished on the road to liberation. Though these women paved the way for other women to have equal rights and more opportunity, they also paved the way for women to forge ahead in an attempt to prove that they can have it all, be it all, and sometimes know it all. Women jumped on the performance track and have never looked back. Sometimes what looks like liberation can be a new bondage, lurking beneath the surface of our lives.

We became free to find our significance through others and through what others thought of us. We became free to strive for beauty, even though the beauty we are hoping for never quite meets reality. And in becoming liberated, educated, and beautiful, we then became free to starve or binge ourselves to death.

We as American women have the highest rate of divorce, depression, and suicide of any nation. Yet we live in a free country—a country that is affluent, beautiful, and liberated. But because it is so liberated, it has almost become oppressive. In redefining our roles we have just about lost ourselves in the maze of perfection and performance.

Women, "we have come a long way, baby!" But the path we now travel has taken us far from the truth in God's Word and far from His original design for us, which is to know the true and living God and be made beautiful in the splendor of His holiness. There is something wrong with this picture. There must be something more. And there is more.

Define: *to state the nature of a thing, to outline clearly, to bring distinction to*

Liberate: *to set free, especially from control of an authority that is thought to be oppressive*

1. **Read Galatians 3:1-3 and 15-29.**

In the first verse of Galatians 3, Paul called the Galatians foolish. He knew they were trying other things in an effort to find fulfillment and peace with God.

∽ What is this saying to you?

∽ Of what does verse 22 say you are a prisoner?

∽ Before faith in Christ came, by what were you held prisoner?

∽ What do verses 28-29 say about your new position as one in Christ? How does this define you now?

2. **Read Galatians 4:1-9.**

∽ According to verses 4-5, what happened within you because God sent His Son?

∞ What was put into your heart (verse 6), and what is your new title?

Now this is a liberating truth; He has set us free, called us His daughters, and given us full rights to the things of the Spirit! Christ has given our lives definition! Woman, you really are loosed!

Reflect for a moment on what your life was before you knew God. For those of you who think you always knew God, then think about the time He became real to you and what you were like before that reality. For, Galatians 4:8 says, "Formerly, when you did not know God, you were slaves. . ."

I certainly was a slave to my own pleasures. Actually, that is all life was about—ME. What would satisfy, promote, encourage, or take care of me. Me, Me, Me. That is life according to the selfish sinful nature. And for some, that may be what they are calling a liberated life. Scripture, however, always gives us the bottom line, and here we see that kind of lifestyle is not liberated but selfish. Living for "self" is not God's outline for our lives.

We all have selfishness—we were born with it—and we need to submit to God in order to be free from it. Unfortunately, as Christians we often start our new life in Christ on the right foot. We are excited, our lives are surrendered to God, and we are going full speed ahead. Then, something happens. Our direction shifts just slightly. We are pulled in the wrong direction. We have gained some spiritual strength and knowledge, so now we try to take over and add to the growth in our own effort.

We begin to struggle with all the things we formerly struggled with. We become selfish Christians, bless-me Christians, and sadly, in becoming this new breed of Christians, we have missed out on the greatest blessing and adventure in life—being hid in Christ, crucified with Him, yet alive and operating in power.

∞ What does Galatians 4:9 speak to you regarding this?

Remember, a slave is held down, restricted, and unable to move about freely. Does this sound like God's will for you, when it is He who said, "If the Son sets you free, you will be free indeed"? (John 8:36)

3. Write out Galatians 2:20.

Indeed, I have been crucified with Christ. My ego is no longer central. It is no longer important that I appear righteous before you or have your good opinion, and I am no longer driven to impress God. Christ lives in me. The life you see me living is not "mine," but it is lived by faith in the Son of God, who loved me and gave himself for me. I am not going to go back on that.

Is it not clear to you that to go back to that old rule-keeping, peer-pleasing religion would be an abandonment of everything personal and free in my relationship with God? I refuse to do that. (Gal. 2:20-21, TM).

This is true liberation for women!

∞ Is your ego still central today? Why?

∞ Are you motivated to action by trying to impress others? Why?

∞ Do you realize the implications of what it means that Christ lives in you? Explain.

When Paul wrote the letter to the Christian churches in Galatia, he did so because the Christians were becoming confused with what the Judaizers were teaching them. The Judiazers were false teachers, who were teaching that Christians were not really saved unless they obeyed every detail of the law. Paul wanted the Christians to know that going back to dependence on the law for salvation would be like fastening ourselves to a ball and chain. It would not produce in us the kind of freedom that Christ intended to accomplish for us on the cross and through giving us His Spirit. He wanted Christians to understand the Spirit's power and to live by faith in Christ. In doing so, they would keep in step with the Spirit, and God could do mighty things in their midst.

But much like us, the Galatians were foolish, and kept reverting to the things that would bind them up. Listen, dear daughter of the Lord, Jesus came to take you out of captivity. He came that you might have life in Him, movement in Him, peace in Him, faith in Him, and confidence in Him. Don't refuse His free gift of grace. Don't refuse the One who wants to bring the key to the locked-up parts of you and set you free. You will never be free until you trust in God's power to unlock and deliver.

A truly free life is one lived in step with God's Spirit, accepting and embracing who I am in Christ, accepting and embracing the others He has created, and most importantly, accepting and embracing *who He is*.

4. Write out John 1:12-14.

∞ To what did Jesus give you the right (or the liberation)?

I love the description of Christ as "the one and only." That is what He is to me and to my road to freedom. He is the one and only way to true, lasting freedom. He is my liberation! I encourage you to take a look at your life and ask yourself: "Am I living as if Jesus is my one and only?"

Remember, God wants what is best for you. Freedom and salvation are the best offer that has ever been made, and they should go hand in hand. If you have accepted Christ for your salvation, you

> *The LORD sets prisoners free, the LORD gives sight to the blind, the LORD lifts up those who are bowed down, the LORD loves the righteous (Ps. 146:7–8).*

now need to accept Him for your freedom. The time is now! Freedom is yours! Take hold of what Christ alone has provided for you. Take it today!

5. Some of us have come to believe that it is God who spoils our plans and is an oppressive, restrictive force in our lives. This is a wrong view of God. It is the world's view, and it is tainted by the oppressor himself—Satan.

Oppress: *to treat with continual cruelty or injustice; to weigh down with cares or unhappiness; to make life difficult to endure*

Real liberation comes when we are free from the oppressive control that the enemy of our souls tries to use to twist and turn our freedom into a horrid bondage once again. He is the oppressor. Oppression is the exact opposite of what Jesus came to do.

∞ Read John 10. What is Jesus referring to here in this chapter?

∞ Why didn't the people understand what He was trying to say?

∞ What does verse 9 say will be the ability of the sheep? Do they move freely? What will they find?

∞ Look up *pasture* in the dictionary and write the definition here.

∞ What is the significance of animals being able to graze freely and be fed?

∞ How can this apply to your life?

∞ What is the overview, main theme, or main statement of John 10?

6. Write out John 10:10.

∞ What are the three objectives and the purpose of the thief?

At night, sheep were often gathered into a sheepfold to protect them from thieves, weather, or wild animals. The sheepfolds were caves, sheds, or open areas surrounded by walls made of stones or branches. The shepherd often slept in the fold to protect the sheep.

In the sheepfold, the shepherd functioned as a gate, letting the sheep in and protecting them. Jesus is the gate to God's salvation for us. He offers safety and security.[1]

The thief here is a picture of what Satan is to us, God's sheep. God offers protection, but Satan is working toward taking from us anything good and right for the purpose of deceiving us into living apart from God in our own strength and effort.

We see Satan pictured as a thief and a wolf. He is also described as a roaring lion ready to devour. He doesn't want you liberated in the Spirit of Christ!

7. Write out 1 Peter 5:8.

∞ What are the two words that are used to describe Satan here?
1.
2.

∞ What are the two things he does?
1.
2.

∞ Read 1 Peter 5:9. What are the two things you are to do in response to who he is?
1.
2.

Are you standing firm in your faith today? Did you know that faith is the thing that will liberate you? Faith in God sets you free from anxiety, obsessiveness, compulsiveness, regrets of the past, worry for today, and negative projection of tomorrow. Faith sets us free and liberates every part of us to be the women that God has designed for us to be.

A woman of faith is truly a liberated woman! She is confident in her place and position in life. She realizes she has value and purpose, and she embraces both in the same way she embraces God. A spiritually liberated woman is free enough to live with passion and joy. She is a woman whose life is defined by a love for Christ and a surrender to His purposes. But instead of being liberated, many continue living in oppression. Some oppression coming straight from the pit of hell, and some stirring up from the fleshly nature within.

8. Read James 4:1-10.

Women are known for gossip, pettiness, jealousies, and other ridiculous actions that are absolutely pathetic, especially for mature adults. What does this passage say causes some of these fights among us?

∞ What is the root problem that causes our inner turmoil? (Hint: it starts with a "P.")

∞ Reflect for a moment on the last time you had a conflict, quarrel, or fight with someone.

• What was battling within you at the time?

• What did you stoop to, in order to get what you wanted?

• Were you behaving as one liberated by Christ, or as one held captive by her own flesh, jealousy, bitterness, insecurity, or pride?

9. Once again let's look at Galatians 6:4.

Make a careful exploration of who you are and the work you have been given, and then sink yourself into that. Don't be impressed with yourself. Don't compare yourself with others. Each of you must take responsibility for doing the creative best you can with your own life (Gal. 6:4, TM).

As we saw in the previous lesson, women are also known for the practice of comparing themselves with other women. We dress for other women, decorate for other women, and act in ways that will impress other women. How sad! As long as we are in the bondage, and yes it is a bondage, of comparing ourselves with other women, we will never be fully liberated in Christ.

He did not create us to be cookie-cutter Christians, or Stepford Christian women! He created each of us unique and individually beautiful in His sight. Stop making excuses for who you are. Embrace God, then embrace the way He formed you, and the way He wired you together . . . every part of you is part of His purpose. You have gifts and abilities all nestled within your own personal package that the woman next to you doesn't quite have. And she has a package that you don't quite have. Both are packages created by God for His purposes. When we quit comparing with others, we become free—liberated—no longer held back or tied down to anyone's expectations. We also become liberated in the deepest parts of us, for we become free to be all that God has called us to be as His woman! In the last lesson, while looking up *compare* in the dictionary, I ran into the definition of *comparison*. Listen to this definition: not comparable because one is so much better than the other.

This is a trap that we can fall into as women. When we compare ourselves with others, we usually think everyone else is so much better that we feel inferior. Then we plummet quickly into thinking that we don't have much worth, and then we go deeper still into the negative seas, thinking we can't be used by God because we are just not as good as others. All three of these thoughts are contrary to God's Word and God's truth!

∞ If you were to base your life on liberating biblical truth, could it be true that you don't have much worth? Explain.

Woman of Wonderful Worth

Everyone of us needs definition in the area of identity. For far too long a woman's identity has been wrapped up in what she looks like, how she acts, how she performs, or who she's connected to. When in reality, what the most important thing is who she is. That's right—who she is.

Do you know who you are?

Not what you do, to whom you are related, or who you would like to be, but who you are.

Unfortunately, most of us don't recognize the beauty and truth of who we are in Christ.

Woman, return to relationship with Christ so that you can find out who you are in Him. If you have never been in relationship with Christ, then enter in—the welcome mat is out. He is calling you to know Him and be liberated by the only power and truth that can set you free.

Remembering Who You Are

10. You are a woman created by God.

∞ Write out the following verses. (Try personalizing them. Your name plugs in perfectly!)

• Psalm 139:13

• Genesis 1:27

• Revelation 4:11

11. You are a woman created for God.

∞ Write out the following verses.
   • Psalm 119:73

   • Psalm 139:16

   • Jeremiah 1:5

   • Colossians 1:16

12. You are a woman protected by God.

∞ What do the following verses mean to you personally?
   • Psalm 139:5

   • John 10:27-28

13. You are a woman created by God.

∞ Write out the following verses.

• John 3:3-8

• John 14:15-18

14. You are a woman with a Father—Abba/Daddy.

∞ What does Romans 8:15-17 mean to you personally?

15. You are a liberated woman—free to be all God has designed you to be *in Him*.

∞ Read Ephesians 1–3. Circle each "in Him" that you come across.
∞ What is the significance of these "in Hims"?

∞ What is this speaking to your heart? Journal your thoughts.

Perhaps you have known Christ for a very long time. You have walked with Him, served Him, and trusted in His Word. But now you find yourself bound up in some tangled mess of indescribable chains, and you do not feel the freedom that you know you have been richly given. I call this being in a funk! Have you ever been there? Sort of under the weather, spiritually and emotionally, worn-out, washed-up, held down and back. I have certainly been in a funk on many occasions. It is especially in these times that I need to remind myself of:
    • who God is,
                • who I am in Christ,
                            • what life is about.

The verses you have looked up, written out, and journaled about in this lesson are good for you to remember. You are His beloved, and His banner over you is love! That banner flies high each day, waving new each morning. Oh that we would trust in His love, for it is is the outline that defines our inner beauty, which says who we really are in the deepest part of our being.

Dear Lord,

I thank You that You are the One who defines me as a woman. I don't have to get swallowed up by other people's expectations or standards, but instead I can trust You with all of me. Father, show me the path to liberation, as I turn my focus on You daily. Amen.

HE IS MY COURAGE

Being Inwardly Renewed Day by Day

Oh no! Not another day, I thought as I pulled the blankets up tightly over my head. In the darkness below the covers I could hide and pretend, even if just for a moment, that my life was back to normal. But once the reality of another day hit me, it was all over. Again I would have to admit that I wasn't in a bad dream or a terrible nightmare, but this was now my life. As soon as I inched my way to the bathroom, I could see that the mirror still reflected swollen eyes and that the pain of a broken heart was still etched on my tired face. I was caught in a real life crisis, and now I needed God more than I ever had.

Would He be real to me now? Could He pave the way for freedom in a life so tightly bound with the chains of fear and worry? What about my broken heart? Did He have the glue to put me back together again?

Maybe like me, you have found yourself saying, "Oh no! I can't believe this is happening!" Perhaps you have lived through disappointments, broken promises, and shattered dreams. Maybe you have suffered loss or financial hardship. Whatever it is, when it strikes you down, it's sometimes hard to recover.

In this lesson we will see that we are not alone in our suffering. Problems are nothing new, but having a new attitude in the middle of the problem can make all the difference in the world. Christ offers the wholeness and the completeness that we are all looking for, regardless of our circumstances. Whether you are strolling along Main Street U.S.A. with everything in order, or you are walking down the Boulevard of Broken Dreams, crushed and afraid, Jesus has the answer for you. He gives us grace in our less than perfect lives. He gives us the courage we need to face another day. He gives us the courage to live in the truth, believe the truth, and act on the positive truth instead of the negative.

> It is not events either past or present which make us feel the way we feel, but our *interpretation of those events*. Our feelings are not caused by the circumstances of our long-lost childhood or the circumstances of the present. Our feelings are caused by what we tell ourselves about our circumstances, whether in words or in attitudes.[1]—*William Backus and Marie Chapian*

1. Read 2 Corinthians 1:3-6.

∞ Write out verses 3-4, circling *so that*.

∞ What are two descriptions of God in these verses?
   1.
   2.

∞ Look up both of these words in a dictionary and write their meanings here.

∞ Why does He help you in your troubles?

∞ Do you see the importance of understanding "so that"? Explain.

∞ How does this put some purpose in the pain and help you identify the truth in your situation?

The Chains of Pain
by Vicky Minamyer

This pain is such a prison.
I feel trapped within my soul.
Can anybody hear me
As I cry from this dark hole?

These chains are tight, they hold me down
From light and truth and joy.
They rob me from the freedom
And the life I should enjoy.

My eyes are tired and weary
And swollen from the tears.
My strength has turned to weakness;
My hope has turned to fears.

It's then I hear the still small voice
Of comfort and pure love.
I lift my eyes toward heaven
My help comes from above.

My God will break these chains of pain.
He alone is my release.
His grace and hope is endless.
His Spirit brings me peace.

He's the only One who sets me free.
I believe His Word is true
"Be at rest once more my soul
For the Lord's been good to you."

2. Continue reading in 2 Corinthians 1:8-10.

Paul didn't want believers to be uninformed. How I thank God for the honesty of the Apostle Paul! He didn't mince words, cover up pain, or pretend that he was a superhero. He just stated the facts and looked to the truth for answers.

Sometimes it might seem as if life has handed you a lemon. Things look sour. As a Christian, you must realize that though you face hardships and struggles, there are no lemons in your walk with the Lord. There may be hard times, but when you adjust your thinking to the truth of God's Word, standing firmly on truth, your attitude will change and so will you. When resting in God's truth, your attitude will refute the hopelessness of thinking life has just given you another lemon.

Instead, as you walk with Jesus there is always the possibility of being conformed more into Christ's image with each challenge you face. Because of this, even the sour becomes sweet. The circumstance at your door may be very hard, but the change it can produce in your heart may be just the "thing" you have prayed for. Take courage in Christ!

∞ What are some of the honest facts Paul shared in 2 Corinthians 1:8-10?
   1. He was under _____ _____.
   2. The pressure was far _____ ____ _____ ____ _____.
   3. He despaired _____ ___ _____.
   4. In his heart he felt _____ _____ ____ _____.

3. Write out 2 Corinthians 1:9-10.

Paul's life was being renewed because of the attitude of his heart and mind. He had trained himself to see and believe God's purpose in everything. Part of becoming women of courage, despite the world's view of less than perfect lives, is taking on the attitude of dependency and trust in a sovereign, loving God. The Apostle Paul saw that everything happened to him *so that* he would not rely any longer on himself, but on God. What a lesson!

∞ Are you currently in any trouble that you need courage to face? Write out the facts.

∞ What practical steps can you take to move away from fear and move closer to courage in Christ?

4. Write out the definition of *courage*.

In John 10:10 (AMP) Jesus Christ Himself said to His disciples: "I came that they may have and enjoy life, and have it in abundance (to the full, till it overflows)." This word *abundance* in the Greek comes from *perissos*, which implies superior in quality. It also means a life with an advantage, beyond measure. Not enough is said about the quality of our lives as Christian women. We want abundance in quantity, don't we? "O Lord, bless me. Make everything OK for me. Give me. . . ." Quantity has come to mean quality in the American life.

What do I have? What can I get? How can I keep it? But quality, not quantity, is what abundance is all about. Abundance can spring forth even in the middle of pain.

> If you have prayed for God to use your life, don't be surprised when trouble comes. Remember, the trouble is intended to strip you of self-sufficiency, a necessary step before God can use you to the fullest. Many times I prayed for God to help with my circumstances and wondered why things didn't seem to get any better. In retrospect, I can see that God was helping by allowing things to get darker. I wanted Him to change the circumstances. He wanted to accomplish His purpose in the circumstance. When you pray for God to help with your situation and things don't get any better, remember that He knows what He is doing! Just because you can't see His hand doesn't mean He isn't working. He may be using the situation to break that outer shell of self-reliance that keeps the life of Christ from being expressed through your lifestyle. No Christian can ever live to full potential until that happens.[2] —*Steve McVay*

Changed from the Inside Out

5. Write out 2 Corinthians 3:17-18.

∞ What is used to describe the Lord in verse 17?

∞ What is present where the Spirit of the Lord is?

∞ What happens to you as you look to the Lord and His Spirit?

∞ According to these verses, from where does the power come that produces changes within you?

There are a few steps to becoming women of courage, walking in His original design for us.

1. We must embrace Christ.
2. We must have intimate relationship with Christ.
3. We must let go of the past and trust God with our future.
4. We must have continual renewing of our minds.
5. We must daily stand in God's truth and grace.
6. We must rely on the power of God's Spirit and not on ourselves.

> Some individuals are what I call "yesterday people," some are "today people" and others are "tomorrow people." Which are you? Yesterday people are those who have allowed the events of the past to dictate the parameters of their life today. They are also so preoccupied with the past that they are blind to the blessings of today. The past is over, and it's time to become a today and tomorrow person.[3] —*H. Norman Wright*

In His message to Joshua after the death of Moses, God was leading Joshua to have the courage to become a today person: "Now then, you and all these people, get ready to cross the Jordan River into the land I am about to give to them—to the Israelites" (Joshua 1:2). God gave Joshua a message to spur him to move on. (Sometimes we need similar encouragement to move on from our pasts.) Then three times God made a statement to Joshua that He is also making to each of us: **"Be strong and courageous."**

6. Embrace Christ.

Embrace: *to hold closely*

☞ Read 2 Corinthians 1:15-20.

Every promise in God's Word is for you, His daughter. Don't get stuck in the trap of thinking they are for "someone else." Apply God's Word to your life, hold on to His promises, don't intellectualize them away because if you do, you will be more like the cowardly lion then like the woman of courage God is shaping you to be.

☞ Write out Psalm 52:8-9.

☞ What three things are you to do to embrace God?
   1.
   2.
   3.

Trusting in God's unfailing love is embracing who He is!

☞ Read on in 2 Corinthians 1:21-22. Who makes us stand firm?

☞ What has Christ done for you?
   1.
   2.
   3.

I challenge you to embrace the Christ who has done for you that which you could not do for yourself.

∞ How does it make you feel to know the three things from the passage above that God has provided for you?

7. Develop an intimate relationship with Christ.

∞ Read Philippians 3:7-10.

Intimate: *close friendship, private and personal*

∞ What does Paul consider everything that is outside of knowing Christ?

[For my determined purpose is] that I may know Him [that I may progressively become more deeply and intimately acquainted with Him, perceiving and recognizing and understanding the wonders of His Person more strongly and more clearly], and that I may in that same way come to know the power outflowing from His resurrection [which it exerts over believers], and that I may so share His sufferings as to be continually transformed [in spirit into His likeness] (Phil. 3:10, AMP).

Yes, all the things I once thought were so important are gone from my life. Compared to the high privilege of knowing Christ Jesus as my Master, firsthand, everything I once thought I had going for me is insignificant—dog dung. I've dumped it all in the trash so that I could embrace Christ and be embraced by him. I didn't want some petty, inferior brand of righteousness that comes from keeping a list of rules when I could get the robust kind that comes from trusting Christ (Phil. 3:10, TM).

∞ Where are you at in your journey of relationship with Christ?

∞ Is your relationship intimate? Explain.

∞ What is your determined purpose in life (honestly)?

∞ Read Philippians 3:12-21. Paul wanted to know Christ so how did he go about doing that?

∞ Think on the following statements about Paul. Can you apply them to your life and use them on your journey into deeper relationship?
  • He wanted to become like Him, so he humbled his heart.
  • He didn't trust in himself or perfection, but he took hold of Christ and what Christ did for him.
  • He pressed into Jesus and took hold of God's promises.
  • He didn't look back, but he pressed forward toward the goal.
  • He didn't compare himself with others, but he lived up to what God was doing in him only.

∞ In Philippians 3:17 what does Paul say you have been given?
  A p_ _ _ _ _ _.

∞ Where is your real home?

> Citizen: *a person who has full rights or a reserved place in a country*

∞ Journal your thoughts on Philippians 3:20-21.

> Today is yesterday's tomorrow you worried about, and all is well. If God sends us on stony paths, He provides strong shoes.[4]
> —*Corrie Ten Boom*

8. Renew your mind.

Renewed: *restored to its original state*   Most things in God's Word seem foreign to us. And rightly so—we have spent years thinking one way, and now the Word of God poses another way to view ourselves and our lives. Though foreign, God's way brings freedom and change from within.

> The law of gravity is evident when you drop something causing it to fall straight toward the center of the earth. So it is with the laws governing the relationship between belief and behavior. What you believe affects how you behave.[5]—*William Backus and Marie Chapian*

∞ Write out Romans 11:36.

∞ Now read the verses after that, Romans 12:1-2, connecting the two into one thought. How are you to live?

Your attitudes and actions are directly related to how you view life. How do you view life?

Paul was urging Christians to view life differently. We are to view life in the light of God's love. God is love—that is who He is. When we view life through the lens of love, we become different people, and our lives are transformed by the power of that love. When we live in the love God has for us, we begin to see changes in our lives. Our minds change and our actions change, and the outcome of our lives changes. It is one big circle.

Grasp God's love / Become more secure
Love/Grace provides a different view on which to base life

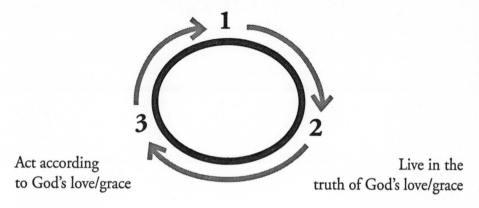

Act according
to God's love/grace

Live in the
truth of God's love/grace

9. Write out Hebrews 13:8.

Firm: *not yielding when pressed, secure, hard, solid*

Stand firm in His Word!

Jesus Christ never changes, yet we change all the time. Rarely are we as firm and secure as we should be. Circumstances wrap themselves around our hearts and minds, and if we are not seeing from the view of love and grace, we will collapse as though God's Word was never spoken to our hearts! If we intend to press toward emotional and spiritual health, we need to be firm and courageous. Do the words *roller coaster* mean anything to you? Women are often on a roller coaster. Blame the ups and downs on hormones if you'd like, but guess what? God has something better! Do you want it?

In emotional and mental health, what you believe is all-important. It makes a difference what you believe. Other people, circumstances, events and material things are not what make you happy. What you believe about these things is what makes you happy or unhappy.[6]—*William Backus and Marie Chapian*

If you want something better out of life, there is one way to get it: fully rely on God! When we rely on God, leaning into His promises, holding on to hope, filling our hearts with courage, then we have peace and strength. Nothing is quite as wonderful as inner peace. This type of peace comes when we rely on the God who created us.

> Anxiety, fear, and worry are the result of our unwillingness to trust God. To worry is the same as saying to God, "I don't believe You."[7]—*Corrie Ten Boom*

10. Rely on God.

∞ Read the following verses, jotting down the key words.
   • 2 Corinthians 3:4-6

   • 2 Corinthians 4:5-7

   • Zechariah 4:6

∞ What did these verses speak to your heart?

11. Read Exodus 3:11-15.

∞ How are you to treat an enemy or someone who has hurt you?

I think sometimes we forget that men such as Moses were just regular people like you and me. Here we see Moses afraid: "Who am I?" And we see God's reply: "I will be with you."

This "I will be with you" is a truth that we must remember. God says that "I AM" is His name forever and that is how He is to be remembered. He doesn't change . . . remember that. He is with us today. It might not seem like it, but part of our courage and mind renewal comes when we put into our mind's little vault precious gems of truth such as "I will be with you."

Dear Lord,

I thank You today that You are working in me each day. Give me courage to face life and all its various seasons. It is because of You that I can bounce back from the messes of life. Your Spirit is like holy elastic to me, giving me stretch-ability. You truly are the One who reclaims my life and renews my mind. May I desire Your Word and intimacy with You more strongly than ever before. Be glorified in my life as I trust in You. Amen.

HE IS MY STRENGTH

Trusting in the God Who Understands My Weaknesses

When it comes to major-league difficulties like death, disease, sin and disaster—you know that God cares. But what about the smaller things? What about grouchy bosses or flat tires or lost dogs? What about broken dishes, late flights, toothaches, or a crashed hard disk? Do these matter to God?

I mean, He's got a universe to run. He's got the planets to keep balanced and presidents and kings to watch over. He's got wars to worry with and famines to fix. Who am I to tell Him about my ingrown toenail?

I'm glad you asked. Let me tell you who you are. In fact, let me proclaim who you are. You are an heir of God and a co-heir with Christ. You are eternal, like an angel. You have a crown that will last forever. You are a holy priest, a treasured possession. You were chosen before the creation of the world. But more than any of the above—more significant than any title or position—is the simple fact that you are God's child. As a result, if something is important to you, it's important to God. Does God care about the little things in our lives? You better believe it. If it matters to you, it matters to him.[1]—*Max Lucado*

1. Read Hebrews 4:14-5:10.

∞ With what in you does God sympathize?

∞ What is an area, or areas, of current weakness in your life?

∞ According to Hebrews 4:16, what are you supposed to do with your area of weakness?

2. Write out Ephesians 3:16.

∞ How do you get power in your inner being?

∞ What do you think of when you think of the word *strong*?

Strength causes me to think of times when I am feeling complete, full of energy, and able to do the tasks set before me. It is a time when I feel empowered and confident.

Naturally, there are times I don't feel strong at all. Those are the times when I, as a woman, cannot open a tightly sealed jar, move a piece of heavy furniture, or fix my broken-down car. There are also times when I feel unsure of myself, afraid to step out in faith and reluctant to join in. I do not feel strong, instead I feel weak.

When I think of *strong*, I think of "being able." To me, strength represents ability and power. Yet often my own ability and power fail me. In fact, quite often I am completely depleted of the strength I need for even the small daily challenges that come my way. Jesus not only wants to give me strength to complete each task, but He also wants to be my strength, my source that wells up from the deepest part of me.

∞ Using a dictionary and a thesaurus, list the meanings of the word *strong*.

> As long as your own abilities are sufficient to rise to the challenge, you will never understand that He doesn't just give strength. He is your Strength. In the breaking process, God has no intention of helping you get stronger. He wants you to become so weak that He can express Himself as the strength you need in every situation.[2]—*Steve McVay*

∞ Circle the definitions in this list below that represent who you are.

able to handle stress	influential
able to handle hardship	sound
firm	straight

In this lesson we will concentrate on God and His Strength. I want us to look at the people we can be, because of Christ's life in us. The first matter of importance is laying the foundation and looking at the originator of strength.

3. Write out Psalm 28:7-8.

∞ In these two verses what words describe the Lord?

We have already looked up *strength* and have seen that it is what makes us capable of exerting effort in any given situation. Strength is what enables us to handle stress, hardship, disappointments, and all of the real things that come into our lives. Strength also enables us to handle blessing and the good stuff in life with humility and honor.

With strength we become sturdy, firm, solid women who can be a positive influence in the world. Each of us lives in her own little corner of the world.

For some of us the corner is very inclusive and small, and for others the borders seem to go on forever. In each case, God can give us the power to be His women of influence as we love Him and walk in the truth of His Word, right where He has placed us. He is living in us.

∞ Record the meaning of the following words as found in a dictionary.

Shield

Fortress

What we can grasp from these few verses in Psalms is quite significant. *Shield* comes from a root word that can be translated defense, deliver from harm, protector, and handling safely over. *Fortress* comes from a root word in the Hebrew that means strong place.

Now, let's stop here and think about what this means to us today. Let's apply this fabulous truth to our own lives.

The Lord is my strength. He is the one who equips me with power to live this life. He is my shield. He protects me, defends me, and delivers me. Because of these two truths, I can trust in Him. When I trust in Him, I am helped and my heart jumps for JOY! Now, that's a switch! Many times my heart is jumping with anxiety over life, not jumping with joy over the provision I have been given to live life with strength and dignity.

The psalmist says that because of these truths he thanks God in song. His heart is bouncing around for joy, his mouth is singing aloud a new song of trust and confidence. Then he states the truth again: "The Lord is the strength of his people, a fortress of salvation for His anointed one" (Ps. 28:8). Think of that . . . a strong place for you, His anointed one.

Now, my friend, open your mouth and let it be filled with thanksgiving to God for His provision for you. Let your mouth be filled with song . . . any song of thanksgiving or praise to your God.

Sit with these two verses—Psalm 28:7-8. Read them over again out loud. Read them as if they were a certified letter you just received in the mail, declaring you as a grand prize winner! Claim that prize today—strength for today and a strong place in which to stand.

> This is what God is for you: *a protector, a defender, a deliver, and a strong place*

∞ Journal your thoughts on these truths and how they can impact your life if you truly believed them.

4. Read Psalm 46.

∞ What are the key thoughts in this psalm?

∞ What are some of the words that describe God?

∞ What are you told to do in verse 10?

To be still means to remain motionless and to be without sound. Apart from sleeping, when was the last time you were completely still—without motion or visual and audible input? Stop right now and be still. Think of only one thing: that He is God. He is who He said He is. Think of just the things you've picked up already in this lesson about His character. Be quiet and still and reflect on these things.

5. In the Bible we see God described as the Creator of heaven and earth and the "God Most High." One of the names of God is El Elyon, the Most High. It is this big, mighty, strong, most high God that has been delivering His people for generations. The following verses will give you a look at your Most High God, your El Elyon. Write out the key thought that speaks to you.

• Genesis 14:20

• Psalm 78:35

God is sovereign. He is the Most High God. He rules and reigns. He is in charge, ladies! We must come to know Him as the Most High Sovereign God if we are ever going to have strength and peace. It is in trusting in His plan that we settle down and rest in Him. This not only gives us strength for today, but it also gives us hope for tomorrow.

∞ What does the truth of Most High God mean to you today?

6. Read Daniel 2:20-23.

∞ For what was Daniel praising God?

∞ What had God given Daniel?

∞ What is the main thought here that can also apply to your life as a person whom God created, just like Daniel?

7. Read Isaiah 46:9-11.

∞ What are the key points in these verses?

∞ What do these verses say to you about God's sovereignty?

Sovereign means supreme ruler. These verses should help establish in your mind the fact that God is the supreme ruler over all things. He has strength and power, doesn't He?

8. Read Psalm 73:23-28.

Verse 23 speaks of God's provision of strength and protection now, as well as the promise of eternal deliverance. In verse 26, we actually get a glimpse of strength despite the loss of health and physical strength. This is a powerful truth, isn't it?

∞ Whom is it good to be near?

∞ What are some of the words that describe God in these verses?

∞ How can you apply these to your relationship with Him?

∞ Write out James 4:8.

∞ What does this verse tell you to do?

∞ What will happen as a result of this action?

∞ Read 1 John 1:8-10. How do you wash your hands and become clean from sin?

∞ Are we all sinners? Why?

9. The remedy for your sin.

∞ Read 1 John 2:1-2 and Matthew 18:21-35.

∞ What is Jesus' message to you on forgiveness?

∞ How does this verse apply to God and our sins?

Remember, God is the strength of your life! He is the forgiver of sins, the giver of power from on high, and the One who protects you from all harm. He is the Strong One on your behalf! But, in order to receive power from on high, you must come near to God. What a concept!

You can't get a lemon from an apple tree or a tomato from a rosebush, and you can't get strength from on high from anyone but the *Most High God!*

∞ Do you draw near to God on a regular basis? Explain.

∞ Write out Isaiah 40:31.

Near: *with little distance between; closely related; to come together with; to be surrounded in*

You have the opportunity to be close to the Most High God—the God of all strength and power. The purpose of that relationship is love. He wants to fill you with strength and power to live, but most of all He desires to fill you with the love of the Father so that you may be full and complete. How can you be filled if you don't come to the well?

My car cannot be filled with gas unless I drive it up to the gas tank and use the pump to fill the car's tank. Just thinking of filling my car will not fill it. Have you ever been on empty, your reserve light shining, and you still procrastinate stopping for gas? What happens if you wait for too long? Bingo!

You are completely empty. You must pull off to the side of the road, and then walk for help and deliverance from this hassle that could have been avoided.

Well, in the same way, if you do not go to God, fill up with His strength each day, you will find yourself on empty. And like your car, maybe you have a reserve tank. But like the car, if you wait for too long, you will be broken down completely, without the fuel you need to function.

Go, my friend, to God! Run to God! Keep your spiritual tank full! There is no cost to this priceless strength, this priceless love, this priceless relationship. Run to God, the Most High Sovereign One! Don't just think about it—do it!

10. How would you describe the opposite of strong?

∞ Look up *weak* in your dictionary and write the definition here.

∞ Read 1 Corinthians 1:26-31. What did God choose?

(Note: Some of you may be very educated, and this verse might seem strange to you. The Apostle Paul was a very educated man too, but the wisdom God can give us is above every system known to man. No one is wise when compared to the Most High God. That's the point.)

11. Write out 1 Corinthians 1:25.

∞ What does this say about strength and wisdom?

∞ Read 1 Corinthians 1:26-31.

∞ What has Christ become for you?

∞ Are you to boast of your own strength, ability, or power? Explain.

12. Read 2 Corinthians 12:1-10.

∞ What is Paul's message to you here?

∞ Write out verses 9-10.

∞ How is this different than your normal attitude about your weaknesses and shortcomings?

∞ Whose power should you desire to rest on you? Why?

As we read through the pages and the history of people in the Bible, we see over and over again the power of God, displayed through men and women's lives. If we are not careful, we can begin to think that the power and the glory were due to the exceptional person that was following God. But, let us not ever forget that the strength, power, and glory all originate and end in God Almighty. People, no matter how greatly used, are just people—like us.

Look at Moses. He started out life as a prince, the son of an Egyptian princess—a privileged existence. But all that changed when he became a shepherd. Now he was living the humble existence of an unknown foreigner and doing the very thing he had despised. From prince to pauper . . . or from prince to regular person . . . this was Moses' lot.

Moses was a person just like you. He was used by God, and we follow his story with awe and wonder. But he was just a person. God was preparing Moses for a great place in leadership even while he was living the life of an unknown Midian shepherd. God knew that Moses would be used to make a difference so God was preparing him for the great things about to happen by allowing Moses to know his own weakness and frailty. Like Moses, when we become aware of our own weakness, we can then recognize more clearly the strength and power of God.

∞ Do you ever feel as if God could never use you? Explain.

∞ Do you recognize your weaknesses and inability to accomplish great things for God in your own strength? Explain.

13. Read Exodus 3:1-15.

∞ What is the message in this passage?

∞ What is this saying to you personally?

Keep in mind that Moses was just a man, as you are just a woman. (Remember, ordinary people do get touched, filled, and used by an extraordinary God!)

Moses felt inadequate. He certainly didn't feel strong, secure, and confident, did he? It was natural for Moses to feel inadequate, because he was not equipped for the job. But God did not ask him to work alone or in his own strength. Just as God gave Moses power so He gives us power, strength, and ability to do His work. We should not look to our own strength, but to the power and providence of God. It is God's way to work through us, as His vessels, to complete His purpose, design, and plan.

∞ In Exodus 3:1-15 what name did God use to describe Himself?

∞ Does this name represent strength or weakness?

∞ What does this say to you?

14. Read Jeremiah 1:4-10.

∞ According to the account of Moses and now Jeremiah, who sends you?

∞ In Jeremiah 1:6 what word describes the Lord?

Here we see the Sovereign Lord again. God is powerful to rule and reign.

∞ What did God do to Jeremiah, and what did God put within him?

∞ Was either Moses or Jeremiah told to go on their own strength, power, or steam? Elaborate.

We might have many great ideas, but they are nothing more than great ideas unless they are brought to fruition by the sovereign plan and power of the Most High God, El Elyon.

Our part is to draw near, to listen for His voice, to watch for His work, to follow in His plan. His part is to produce the power, strength, and the subsequent fruit that will grow as a result of our living in His will and walking in His ways. We abide; He acts.

Many of us don't realize our weakness or our limitations. Self-esteem is good, but only if it is biblically based and balanced. It must be in line with the truth in God's Word. To esteem myself and believe in myself just for "self" sake, is not a biblical or balanced approach to life. But to see myself in Christ and to value my life because Christ has plans and purposes for me to walk in is quite a different reality. In this reality, I see myself as a woman empowered by God. Recognizing my weaknesses doesn't stop me for I know that with God all things are possible, and in God is all strength and power. I realize that the outcome totally rests on God's power, not on my performance.

15. Read Joshua 1.

∞ What is the main theme in this chapter?

∞ What instruction does God give Joshua?

∞ What does verse 5 say that speaks of the abiding of God's power and strength in your life?

∞ How many times do you find the phrase "Be strong and courageous" in this chapter?

∞ Why do you think this phrase was repeated so many times?

∞ Write out Joshua 1:9.

In this verse we are given the key to being strong in the Lord. We are told, "Be strong and courageous." We are also told not to be terrified or discouraged. How can we walk in this kind of strength? We walk in this strength by having faith in the fact that the Lord God will be with us wherever we go! If we really believed that God was always with us, and that we were never alone, we would have no need for fear. We would also not let our weaknesses and inadequacies get us down, for we would be conscious of the fact that the power of God rests on us, always at work within us, enabling us to walk in the Spirit and to do the will of God.

∞ In your dictionary look up the following three words and record their meaning.

- *terrified*

- *discouraged*

- *courageous*

⤷ What do these definitions say to you as you begin to put together the practicality of the message here in Joshua?

16. Write out Exodus 14:13-14.

> *I have strength for all things in Christ Who empowers me [I am ready for anything and equal to anything through Him Who infuses inner strength into me; I am self–sufficient in Christ's sufficiency] (Phil. 4:13, AMP).*

⤷ What do these verses say to you about God's power, strength, and ability?

⤷ Read Exodus 15:1-13. Journal your thoughts on the power and strength of God and what it means to your life today.

Memorize this verse this week:

> Whatever I have, wherever I am, I can make it through anything in the One who makes me who I am (Phil. 4:13, TM).

Dear Lord,

I need to be focused on Your strength and power rather than on my weakness and inability. All things are possible through You. You work out everything according to Your will, using ordinary human flesh. You use real people such as Moses, Joshua, and Jeremiah. They seem like such big and mighty men to me, but in reality there were just people learning to follow their God. Teach me how to follow You and how to walk in Your strength day by day. Use me as one ordinary woman, empowered by an extraordinary God. Amen.

HE REBUILDS ME

Experiencing the Power That Puts Me Together Again

Smoke filled the skies, settling into the valley like a dark cloud. What started out as a carefree Sunday soon turned into a catastrophic tragedy that turned many people's lives upside down as their homes and cherished possessions were reduced to ashes within just a few short hours. From a distance we could see the hills left charred and covered with the debris that would tell the story of disaster for many months to come. It was an awful picture, but the ruins of those hills and those homes is not where the story ends. Rather than ending abruptly, leaving nothing but loss, the story continues as the people move into the phase of rebuilding and restoring that which was lost.

Our lives are often like a house, destroyed by the devastating heat and flames of fire. We might not know the how or why, but within each of us are areas that are broken, bruised, or completely burned. We need God in His might and wisdom to rebuild our lives.

> Change is possible for you if you have a relationship with Jesus Christ. Why? Because faith in Christ is a life of continuing inward change that leads to outward change. Allowing Him to change us on the inside is the starting point. Paul wrote, "I am again in the pains of childbirth until Christ is formed in you" (Gal. 4:19). He was telling us that we must let Jesus Christ live

> in and through us. When you grasp the fact that Christ is working inside you, your hope will soar for the changes you desire to make.[1]—*H. Norman Wright*

1. In the following definition of *rebuild*, circle any word that might describe the work you need God to do in your life right now.

to build again after destruction	return
restore	revive
reestablish	reclaim
reinstate	recondition
renew	rejuvenate
refresh	

☜ Journal your thoughts on the rebuilding work of Christ in your life.

☜ Write out Psalm 30:11-12.

In this lesson we are going to look at some of the different works of rebuilding in our lives as women.

2. *Rebuild* means to reinstate.

Each of us needs to reinstate our reliance on Almighty God. Let's look at Nehemiah to see how the act of reinstatement is the first step in the process.

☜ Read Nehemiah 1.

We must notice three things in this Nehemiah passage.
1. Verse 3—The people are in great trouble; the wall has been broken and burned.

2. Verse 6—They confess their sin, the first step toward rebuilding.

3. Verses 4,10—They remember God's covenant of love, His redemption, and His strength.

So here we can see our need for:
• acknowledgment of our condition,
• action towards our sins,
• acceptance of His love.

Clarity, Confession, Covenant

∞ What was the condition of Jerusalem?

∞ Are you now, or have you ever been in a broken-down condition? Explain.

∞ Have the gates of your heart been burned or altered by life circumstances? Explain.

∞ Have you experienced God and His goodness, only to walk away from Him? Why?

Nehemiah admitted that the people in Jerusalem had not always been right before God, yet he knew that they were God's people, and he believed that God redeems His people by His strength and might. He prayed the prayer of confession and began to embrace God's covenant of love. It is because of God's love for His people that broken hearts and lives can be rebuilt.

God can rebuild your life. Perhaps you have been brought to ground level. Rubble is all around you—the debris of a life that hasn't met your expectations. For many the rubble is the aftermath of years of negative influence and thinking. It may have started subtly, but the fire erupted and caused widespread destruction. God not only has the strength to rebuild you, but He also desires to redeem you by His might. Reinstating God as your Sovereign Lord is the place to begin. Remember the "LORD, God of heaven, the great and awesome God, who keeps His covenant of love" (Neh. 1:5).

3. *Rebuild* means to reestablish.

It is easy to forget the goodness of God to be faithful in the rebuilding process. We must remember that rebuilding is a process, completed brick by brick. Often during the process it may seem as if things are anything but smooth. We now must establish firmly in our minds two truths.

1. There is a God in heaven who redeems and rebuilds by His great strength.
2. There is an enemy that attempts to stop the process of the rebuilding work.

Nehemiah desired to see God's people blessed and rebuilt, just as Jesus desires to bless and rebuild His people.

∞ But what happens in Nehemiah 2:10, especially in regard to Sanballat and Tobiah?

4. Look at Nehemiah 2:17-20.

People in trouble . . . in ruins.
Rebuild . . . no longer a disgrace.
Rebuilding is a good work of God.
Satan has no claim or right to the one God is rebuilding.

∞ What are these verses saying to you and the rebuilding that God desires to do in your life?

5. Read 2 Corinthians 4:7-18.

Here we read that there is an all-surpassing power at work in us, but it is not of us, it is of God. According to His divine plan, God made us out of ordinary material; we are like jars of clay, which could crumble. And there is a purpose in this plan: to reinstate us as people who live by the power of God, not in our own small strength. Why would we want puny strength, when we could have God's strength? Why would we want to rely on ourselves, limited and able to crumble, when we can put our full reliance on God, who not only gives us strength but also imparts stability?

Not only do we need to establish our reliance on Christ, but we also need to be reminded constantly, and cement within our thought pattern, the truth that God has a purpose in all of life's events. His purpose is to conform us into His image . . . to rebuild or reinstate us, according to the resurrection power at work within each believer in Jesus Christ. We see in this passage how Paul did not rely on himself but on Christ. He knew that he belonged to Christ (a reinstated life). He also knew that despite his trials he was God's (established life).

6. Based on 2 Corinthians 4:8-9, complete the following chart.

Present Circumstance	*Response of one established in Christ*
1. hard pressed on every side	not crushed
2.	
3.	
4.	

Now, fill in the following with your true present circumstances and your desired, reestablished response.

Present Circumstance	*Reestablished Response in Christ*
1.	
2.	
3.	
4.	

∞ What do the phrases "death at work" and "life at work" in 2 Corinthians 4:12 mean to you?

∞ Which is at work in your life? Why?

∞ What truths keep Paul going in spite of all his hardships?

∞ Why do you think God allowed Paul to go through so many hard things?

When God reinstates something, He restores it to its original position. We see here that it was God's plan to make us ordinary so that He can shine as the extraordinary God that He is, reinstating His power through our lives daily. But how many of us are OK with ordinary? We live in a culture that pushes us to be more than ordinary. God wants to reinstate His truth in our lives. The truth is clear, but we don't hear it. We were not created to be "special," but we were created for His purposes. And guess what? That, my friend, is a special, extraordinary purpose! Part of rebuilding is coming back to God's original blueprints and reinstating the original plans.

7. *Rebuild* means to restore.

Each of us has the privilege and right to restoration because of the work of Jesus Christ on the cross. He came to restore us, but there is always a battle of discouragement while we await His work in our lives.

∞ Read Nehemiah 4:1-3.
∞ What happened once the work of rebuilding actually started?

∞ Do you think the enemy of your soul is mocking and angry when he sees the work of God going on in your life? Why?

∞ What five questions was Sanballat asking?

8. Read Nehemiah 4:4-23.

∞ Describe the opposition to the good work of restoration and rebuilding.

∞ How does this relate to your life?

∞ Write out Nehemiah 4:14.

Notice what this verse says we are to do.
1. Resist fear.
2. Remember God.

∞ What does Nehemiah 4:20 say?

9. Read Psalm 23.
This psalm declares the beauty of a love/trust relationship with a God who tenderly watches over us.

∞ What are some of the things that the Lord does? (e.g., He makes me lie down.)

∞ What was the psalmist's response to this loving Shepherd?

I will _____

I will_____

Don't wrestle, just nestle.—*Corrie Ten Boom*

Because of the nature of the Shepherd, we can make life choices that are in proper response to the amazing love of God toward us who believe. We can work with all of our hearts toward that which is right for us—just as the Jews worked at the rebuilding of the wall, through constant trust in the power of God, the God of might, and the God of love.

Do you see how the work of the shepherd in Psalm 23 displays the restorative work of God? Do you feel any indication of renewed vigor or renewed direction as a result of a look at the Lord as your shepherd?

restore:
renewed vigor

10. Write out Psalm 23:3.

The word *soul* sounds so spiritual that sometimes I don't think we get in touch with what it is . . . in real terms. When I think of my soul being restored, I sometimes picture the religious part of me being made better for the purpose of religious tasks. But that is not true restoration. Rather than some lofty, unapproachable concept, the restoring of one's soul is very practical and quite necessary. Since we depend on our minds and our emotions much of the time, they need to be restored and built up with the truth of God and His Word. We have been influenced by our pasts, our culture, and the way in which we lived and built our lives before Christ. Now, we must be influenced by God. Surely, He will lead us in paths of righteousness!

11. *Rebuild* means to rejuvenate.

Scripture tells us that those who wait on God will renew their strength and are likened to eagles in flight. Part of the rebuilding is the work of infusing us with renewed strength.

☞ Write out Psalm 51:10-12.

rejuvenate:
to restore vigor to

☞ In these verses do you see how restoring the joy of your salvation would be like adding fresh new vigor to your life? Explain.

∞ Do you need a spiritual spring to your step? Elaborate.

I encourage you to make these verses a prayer. These verses speak of a life laid down, and a life being rebuilt, or rejuvenated, by the power of God's Holy Spirit.

12. Read Psalm 51:13-19.

∞ What is the response of a person after being restored or rejuvenated? (v. 13)

∞ What are the sacrifices that God receives from you?

The word *broken* here comes from the Hebrew *shabar*, which means burst in pieces, bring to birth, crush, destroy.

∞ Look up the word *broken* in a dictionary and record the meaning here.

∞ Does God despise or turn away that which is broken?

∞ What does He do? (v. 18)

Though God does allow us to be broken, He is faithful to meet every need as He builds us up again. Each of us has three very specific needs in common.

1. The need to belong.

2. The need to be unique.

3. The need to be needed.

> When these needs aren't filled, we experience a terrible emptiness. When they are filled, we find joy and delight. These unfulfilled needs and their accompanying emptiness are not sins and they're not tragedies. They are gifts to us from God. All fulfillment and all pleasure begin with emptiness; without emptiness there is no awareness of need and no capacity to be filled. He has created our needs in order to meet them.[2]—*Dr. Verle Bell*

Broken isn't necessarily bad. Broken puts us in position to be rebuilt. When we are built up in the Holy Spirit, our lives will be forever changed!

> God will take events and intervene to accomplish His purpose. But God also will initiate circumstances that will cause us to depend upon Him and acknowledge Him as we never have before.[3] —*Cynthia Heald*

Dear Lord,

Thank You for making every provision for me long before I ever had the thought of asking for Your provision. You have equipped me with everything I need for life. It amazes me that You give me instruction for the most practical things, and even the smallest detail that doesn't seem like it would matter. You are there even in the tiny stuff—holding me, helping me, healing me, and rebuilding my walls. Please continue Your construction, making me all You have planned. Amen.

HE WORKS IN ME

Getting to the Heart of Me

God loves you just the way you are, but he refuses to leave you that way. He wants you to be just like Jesus.

When my daughter Jenna was a toddler, I used to take her to a park not far from our apartment. One day as she was playing in a sandbox, an ice-cream salesman approached us. I purchased her a treat, and when I turned to give it to her, I saw her mouth was full of sand. Where I intended to put a delicacy, she had put dirt.

Did I love her with dirt in her mouth? Absolutely. Was she any less my daughter with dirt in her mouth? Of course not. Was I going to allow her to keep the dirt in her mouth? No way. I loved her right where she was, but I refused to leave her there. I carried her over to the water fountain and washed out her mouth. Why? Because I love her.

God does the same for us. He holds us over the fountain. "Spit out the dirt, honey," the Father urges. "I've got something better for you." And so he cleanses us of filth: immorality, dishonesty, prejudice, bitterness, greed. We don't enjoy the cleansing; sometimes we even opt for the dirt over the ice cream. "I can eat dirt if I want to!" we pout and proclaim. Which is true—we can. But if we do, the loss is ours. God has a better offer. He wants us to be just like Jesus.[1]—*Max Lucado*

He works in us daily, moving in us and shaping us.

1. Write out Isaiah 58:9.

> **Work:** *mix, form, shape, to perform a function effectively, to operate, to use one's influence on, to bring gradually to a more developed state, to advance.*

In the last lesson we saw that Nehemiah was known to be a man of prayer. He prayed to confess his sins, he prayed for God's help, and he prayed for his enemies.

∞ Make a list of what you need to pray for in your "heart's" current project.

∞ What dirt do you need to spit out at God's water fountain?

2. Read Isaiah 58:11-12.

∞ What does this passage say the Lord will do for you?
  1.
  2.
  3.

∞ What will you be like?

∞ What will happen when you go to the Lord for help?

∞ What are some descriptions of what will happen to you by God's power in Isaiah 58:11-12?
  1. The Lord will_____me always.
  2. He will _____ my needs.
  3. He will _____ my frame.

4. The ancient ruins (caused by the hurt, debris, and baggage) of my life will be _____.

3. Read Isaiah 59:1-2.

∞ What separates you from God and hinders the work of rebuilding?

∞ What happens when you live with unconfessed sin?

You must stay connected to the Lord, your strength, if you are going to be reconditioned by Him and rebuilt by His Spirit.

4. Write out the following verses.
• Psalm 127:1

• Proverbs 14:1

Clarity of condition: *acknowledge your current condition*
Confession of sin: *turn from the sin associated with your condition*
Covenant of love: *embrace God's love for you and live in freedom*

• Proverbs 24:3-4

A wise woman knows that confession is a major step in rebuilding.

A foolish woman ignores God's plan and tries to build with her own wisdom. Let's look closer.

Clarity: clearness

∞ Humble yourself before God, asking for wisdom from Him. What needs rebuilding?

∞ What is broken?

∞ What does He desire to do in your life?

∞ What is your current condition?

∞ Write out Proverbs 24:14.

Confession: a statement of one's wrongdoing

∞ Look up the following verses.
  • 1 John 1:9-10—Confess He is faithful to forgive.
  • Isaiah 58:9—Confess and you will not live in separation.
  • James 5:16—Confess to others and be healed.

Covenant of love: a formal agreement or contract

∞ Read the following verses.
  • Isaiah 58:9
  • Jeremiah 31:3-4

∞ Because of His love, what does He say when you cry for help in your broken places?

5. Read Jeremiah 31—the entire chapter.

Notice God's promise to rebuild and restore. Underline verses that speak to you. Circle words that are key to heart application. Personalize the meaning in the message.

∞ What is this chapter saying to you?

Today God says, "I am here for you, precious daughter." He longs to build you up, make you strong, fill you with rare and beautiful treasures that only His Spirit can give you.

6. Read Nehemiah 9:1-16.

∞ What is this saying about the Israelites?

∞ Write out Nehemiah 9:17.

∞ Read Nehemiah 9:19-31.

∞ What were the Israelites like?

∞ How did God look after them?

∞ Did they remain faithful? Explain.

∞ What happened when they were too comfortable?

∞ Do you ever need your faith renewed when you get too comfortable? Elaborate.

∞ What does verse 28 say that relates to your life today?

∞ Can you relate to needing deliverance time after time? Why?

∞ Write out Nehemiah 9:31.

Nehemiah 9:32 says that God keeps His covenant of love. Part of rebuilding is being renewed in this truth.

∞ How is God described in Nehemiah 9:32?

∞ What does He keep?

7. Read 2 Corinthians 5:16-18.

∞ What did God do for you?

Part of the rebuilding is having God establish you, making you secure in who you are in Him. Pray for a renewed mind!

So we're not giving up. How could we! Even though on the outside it often looks like things are falling apart on us, on the
inside, where God is making new life, not a day goes by without his unfolding grace. These hard times are small potatoes
compared to the coming good times, the lavish celebration prepared for us. There's far more here than meets the eye. The
things we see now are here today, gone tomorrow. But the
things we can't see now will last forever (2 Cor. 4:16-18, TM).

8. Write out Romans 12:2.

Do you think the changing of your mind, thought, and attitude patterns
has anything to do with God rebuilding you from the inside out, at the very
heart of you? Explain.

If you take a glass jar, punch some air holes in the lid, and put
several flies inside the jar, they will fly around and around des-
perately trying to find a way out of their prison. If the lid has
been on for sometime, the result is fascinating: When you take
it off, the flies stay in the jar. That's right, they won't try to get
away. The opening is clear, and all they have to do is fly up and
out. But they won't. They will circle in the same pattern inside
the jar. When they get close to the opening, they fly back down
again. They continue to reenact their pattern of frustration and
imprisonment even though they are only inches from being free.
People are no different. We also fly around in the painful ruts of
the past. And even when the lid is off and the possibility of
being set free is before us, we often remain.[2]—*Leonard Felder*

∞ Do you think you have patterns affecting you? How so?

∞ What is an area of your mind that needs to be renewed right now?

In Romans 12, we see clearly that we are not to pattern ourselves after the rules or general customs of the world we live in. Instead, we are to be changed in character by having our minds made new. This transformation changes our voltage! I don't know about you, but at times, I could use a bit more energy and enthusiasm for life. This transformation turns my life right side up.

> Conform: *to keep rules or general customs*
> Transform: *to make a great change in the character of, to change the voltage*

> So here's what I want you to do, God helping you: Take your everyday, ordinary life—your sleeping, eating, going-to work, and walking-around life—and place it before God as an offering. Embracing what God does for you is the best thing you can do for him. Don't become so well-adjusted to your culture that you fit into it without even thinking. Instead fix your attention on God. You'll be changed from the inside out (Rom. 12:1-2, TM).

9. Read Nehemiah 6:16, 12:27, 12:43.

The wall of Jerusalem was rebuilt in fifty two days. God's work was ultimately done, and the enemy was defeated. The people of Israel rejoiced and were refreshed in God's love and presence. In the same way, the enemy of your soul is a defeated foe! Can you rejoice?

∞ Explain what these verses mean to you.

10. Read James 4:7-8.

Tobiah and Sanballat could not ultimately ruin or thwart the work of God. His blessing was on the wall being rebuilt. God honored the work, the prayer, and obedience of the people. It may seem to you that your enemies have gained ground in your life. But God is the one who will have the ultimate victory. Now you must follow the directives in James 4:7-8:

1. Submit yourself to God.
2. Resist the devil.
3. Come near to God.

Everyone of us is under construction. We are a work in process, a building that is being constructed piece by piece, beam by beam, inch by inch. In a life filled with quick fixes and instant solutions, we are tempted to think that our spiritual lives should "shape up" with the speed of a microwave dinner. We are hard on ourselves. Instead of accepting the fact that we are under construction and trusting the building to God, we self-destruct by allowing negative and untrue thoughts and patterns to grow unexamined and unchallenged. There are many lies that are only meant by Satan to devour and destroy every part of us. Part of our rebuilding is learning the ropes of life on a construction site.

> In [this] freedom Christ has made us free [and completely liberated us]; stand fast then, and do not be hampered and held ensnared (Gal. 5:1, AMP).

I'm sure you've seen a construction site. Hard hats, tool belts, and debris scattered around. We as women who are serious about living in God's abiding power and freedom must also learn to don our hard hats, while always carrying our tools! As we resist the Devil, there might be debris left around our feet, but our most efficient property manager, Jesus, will attend to the rubble. Our goal is freedom in Christ!

11. Read Ephesians 6:10-18.

∞ Where are you to find the strength for a rebuilt life?

∽ What are you to put on? Why?

∽ With what is your real struggle?

∽ Because of this struggle, what are you to wear? Describe the different aspects of the "new outfit."

Full Armor of God

1.
2.
3.
4.
5.
6.

12. Write out Ephesians 6:18.

∽ After trusting in God and putting on your new construction garb, what practical thing are you told to do on all occasions?

∽ What are your thoughts on the armor and the instruction, for those of us who, by the Spirit, are under construction?

∽ Write out Romans 6:4.

∽ What kind of life are you to live?

∞ Has your life changed since knowing Christ? How so?

∞ If your life hasn't changed, does this lesson point out a possible reason why?

Any new structure has to be built on a solid foundation, and construction would have to take place using new materials. In the same way, our lives are being built up again in Christ Jesus. But in order for the building to begin, the proper foundation must be laid.

∞ Romans 6:4 ends with seven powerful words (NIV). What are they?

1.   5.
2.   6.
3.   7.
4.

A new life in Christ is to be our foundation. Coming to Christ and relying on Him should be the very things we base our life on.

13. Write out Matthew 11:28.

Dear Lord,

There is so much work to be done in me. I am glad that I can relax in the truth that You are already working, even though I can't see it or feel it. By faith I believe that You are taking the dirt out of my life and working Your goodness in. While You are building me up, please build me according to Your plan, which is to make me just like You. Amen.

HE IS MY HELP

Looking at Strongholds and His Power to Demolish Them

> God has handed us two sticks of dynamite with which to demolish our strongholds: His Word and prayer. What is more powerful than two sticks of dynamite placed in separate locations? Two strapped together. Prayer keeps us in constant communion with God, which is the goal of our entire believing lives. . . . The ultimate goal God has for us is not power but personal intimacy with Him. Yes, God wants to bring us healing, but more than anything, He wants us to know the Healer.[1] —*Beth Moore*

In this lesson, we will look at what God has made available to us and how His divine help is all-powerful for the pulling down of things that are too big and strong for us. Things like bad habits, dishonoring thoughts, and destructive patterns—the sins that so easily tangle us up.

1. Once again, write out Romans 12:2.

∞ By what pattern are you living?

Pattern:
to model something after a certain design, to use as an example, to arrange by a specific shape or form

It is amazing how quickly patterns develop in our lives. This year while staying in a hotel, I became frustrated after drinking two glasses of warm water from the bathroom sink. I couldn't believe the cold water didn't work because this was such a nice hotel.

Then it hit me. It wasn't the faucet, it was me! I was only reaching for the left handle, the hot water faucet. I hadn't even tried the right faucet. Why? Well, for several months my sink faucets at home were broken and in need of repair. I could only use the left handle, which gave me hot water. Over the months I had learned how to adapt to only using the left side of my sink. Though broken, I learned how to make it work for me.

Now, in a hotel with both faucets working and nothing broken, I still habitually behaved as if I were at home with my broken faucet. I didn't even try to use the right faucet. But when I got the results I didn't want—hot water—I was shocked. Why? I hadn't realized it was my pattern of behavior that produced the wrong results. I was blaming the hotel faucet.

This was a powerful object lesson for me! I was standing in front of a perfectly good, functional sink, and without even thinking I acted as if it didn't work because I was in the habit or pattern of getting by with something broken. Oh, in how many other areas of my life could I possibly be operating this way too?

Sometimes we have patterns or habits in our lives that we do not even realize we have because we are so familiar with them that they now go unnoticed—we are at home with them. Perhaps they are all we have ever known, and we don't realize that God has something better.

The Bible calls fortified, deeply ingrained areas, strongholds (2 Cor. 10:4-5). They are areas that have been strengthened mentally or morally. When Christ holds a strong place in our hearts (Ps. 31:3, Ps. 94:22), it is a good thing. But when sin, ungodly habits, lies of the enemy, messages from the past, or expectations of this world have a stronghold on us, it must be dealt with.

Our minds are like computers. Our brain records all the experiences we have in life. We all were born with very open and malleable minds—little knowledge had been programmed into our computers yet. Many of us were raised with nominal or no knowledge of God, and we learned to live independently of God. Now later in life when we come to Christ, our minds are still programmed to live independently of God. There is no "delete" button to clear our minds, and no "clear" button we can push to get rid of old thinking patterns. Because of this, we have to be constantly reprogramming our minds with the truth in God's Word.

This takes time, attention, and energy. But we shouldn't be discouraged because God gives us everything we need.

When our minds change, our actions change and our lives are different.

2. Look up the following verses and discover some of what God gives you. Write out each verse or your thoughts on each.

- John 14:17 (He gives you the Spirit of truth.)

- John 16:13 (He guides you into all truth.)

- 1 Corinthians 2:16 (You have the mind of Christ.)

- 2 Corinthians 10:3-5 (You have superior weapons for winning the war.)

3. What is a stronghold?

- A stronghold is a negative pattern of thinking that has been burned into our minds either by habitual reinforcement or because of certain life experiences.
- A stronghold is any area of our lives we cannot control, which is destructive.[2]
- A stronghold is an area, causing havoc, which has a strong, powerful hold on us.

∞ Write out 2 Corinthians 10:5.

A stronghold is anything that exalts itself in our minds "pretending" to be bigger or more powerful than our God. It steals much of our focus and causes us to feel overpowered. Controlled. Mastered. Whether the stronghold is an addiction, unforgiveness toward a person who has hurt us, or despair over loss, it is something that consumes so much of our emotional and mental energy that abundant life is strangled—or callings remain largely unfulfilled and our believing lives are virtually ineffective. Needless to say, these are the enemy's precise goals.[3] —*Beth Moore*

Does this verse help you see that a stronghold is an argument against what is good and true for you and your life? Every action or thought that is contrary to God's Word must be demolished! I don't know about you, but there is going to be a lot of crashing going on at my construction site! I have habits and ingrained patterns that have never seen the glory of God. Do you know what I mean? A stronghold is an area that takes over my thinking and dominates me. It is not a fleeting, but a contamination.

Stongholds are those things which control us—they are com-pulsions. Compulsions are those behaviors that we regret doing, but continue doing. No matter how negative these behaviors are to us and no matter how we hate them, we still do them.[4] —*Robert McGee*

Most of us don't take the time to identify our problems, and consequently we don't take the time to address them. Usually we just whine about them, or hide them and feel like a failure as the weakness or problem continues to overtake us. When we never see what we are doing wrong, our strongholds continue to destroy us and the people around us.

The following list outlines some possible areas of strongholds.

Depression	Bitterness	Rebellion	Pride
Sexual Impurity	Fears	Doubt	Anger
Insecurity	Addictions	Occult	Deceit

Most of us have negative messages that hold us down. We don't deal with them; we just let them float around in space. We don't realize that those negative messages are contrary to the truth of God's Word, and they are doing damage! Brain damage, attitude damage, pattern damage, relational damage. And they may have been doing damage for years!

4. In these verses we see that the center of spiritual bondage is in the mind. There is a battle to be won, and it's in our minds.

∞ Look up the following verses.
  • Romans 7:23
  • Romans 8:5-7

∞ What is your mindset?

Since your mind wasn't erased when you became a Christian, there is a battle going on at mind-level. Old habits and old thought patterns that might not be God-honoring fight for attention. Your old patterns were not erased; they are the part of your flesh that must be dealt with on a daily basis. Fortunately, you are new in Christ Jesus.

5. Write out 2 Corinthinans 5:17.

We are now a new work of God's Spirit. Because of His work in our lives, we can deal with old habits and strongholds, and we can have victory over the darkness that they represent. Don't be fooled for a moment . . . old habits are hard to break, and Satan does not give up the fight easily. That is why we can't use weapons that are carnal. We must fight in the power of the Holy Spirit.

What are the weapons that we are to use in this battle of the mind?

In Ephesians 6:10-11 we are told that God has mighty power, and because of this power we can take a stand *in Him*. Ephesians 6 goes on to outline the tools we must use when dealing with areas of darkness.

- *Truth*—This is Jesus Christ Himself and His Word.
- *Righteousness*—This is standing in agreement with the power of the blood of Christ, rather than in our own carnal understanding.
- *Gospel of Peace*—His Word brings peace to the messes of life.
- *Faith*—Believing in God extinguishes the fire of the enemy! Faith pleases God (Heb. 11:6).
- *Salvation*—This is our headgear. We must remind ourselves of our inheritance and what was purchased for us on the cross—our freedom.
- *Spirit*—This is the power and energy powerfully at work in us daily.

When we are abiding in Christ, connecting to Him daily, in relationship with Him, then we are in the full armor of God. Abiding is the key; relationship is the key.

6. Read 2 Corinthians 11:13-14.

Satan doesn't sound an alarm when he is coming to attack us. He doesn't come after us like a bull in a china shop. No! He slithers in like a sneaky snake, waiting and watching to strike us when we are least expecting it. Sometimes he masquerades as something good. Watch out.

As we saw in 2 Corinthians 10:5, we need to bring every thought captive, make every thought subject, to Christ. Patterns and habits are learned behaviors. Some of our learned behaviors are not God's best for us, and once they become ingrained habits, they exercise a strong hold over us. Satan's temptation must be conquered right at the threshold of our minds.

If you don't stop the temptation while in your mind, and instead mull it over, you will open yourself up to possibly acting on this temptation. Once acted on, you may set yourself up for forming a sinful habit. And if you practice a sinful habit long enough, a stronghold will be established in your mind. Once a stronghold is established in any given area, you lose the ability to easily control your behavior in that area. It is then that you feel "out of control." What are you going to do?

So how can you begin to demolish strongholds in your life?

- Identify the lie, the problem, at mind level (all actions start first in the mind).
- Pray, giving it to Jesus.
- Believe Scripture that the fight is not against things you totally understand. Resist Satan! (2 Cor. 10:3-5)
- Begin thinking about things worthy of praise (Phil. 4:8).
- Replace the negative thought or lie with the truth of God's Word.

We may have already prayed for God to eliminate our strongholds, especially the more obvious ones such as anger and depression. When the strongholds aren't immediately destroyed, we assume God answers other people's prayers and not ours. But perhaps God actually wants us to discover that he has provided us what it takes to deal with the problem. We have his Holy Spirit, access to his power and authority, promises from Scripture, and much more. Yet sometimes we are tricked into sitting passively, waiting for God to do every little thing for us, and feeling defeated. We need to learn to take action when action is called for. *Passivity is the Christian's worst problem.*

Satan does all he can to establish a stronghold in your life, but God has given his people the power and authority to demolish those strongholds and run him out. Our life belongs to God but Satan can boldly lay claim to them even though he has no right to do so. We need to identify evil, and handle it God's way.

Many of us women are held captive to insecurity. This keeps us from living fully for God and His plan. It is time to see ourselves as God's daughters and put away the messages that we carry around on our old tapes and labels. Others' opinions are often not God's truth.

∞ To which of the following labels are you most sensitive? Check what applies to you.

Pitiful	Loser	Liar	Never amount to anything
Lazy	Stupid	Incompetent	No one would ever want you
Failure	Freak	Worthless	You should be ashamed of yourself

∞ Of the things you checked, do you still believe that label, and live accordingly? Why?

In every situation we have a choice. We can walk in the Spirit, responding to truth, or walk in the flesh, responding to the patterns we learned to live in before we met Christ. The two are in opposition (Gal. 5:17). If we walk according to "the basic principles of the world," rather than according to Christ (Col. 2:8), we will establish habits that will lead to strongholds.

7. God's emphasis is always the woman within, the inner person.

∞ Look up the following verses, and write out or sum up each one.
• 1 Samuel 16:7

• Proverbs 23:7

• Proverbs 23:12

• Matthew 5:21-22

• Matthew 5:28

∞ Which comes first—thoughts or actions? Explain.

8. **Write out Philippians 2:13-15.**

∞ What do the words *murmuring* and *disputing* mean to you?

9. **Write out the following verses and personalize them.**

• Romans 8:26

> Help: *to make it easier for a person to do something; to aid, assist, relieve, support; to keep something erect, stable, secure*

• 2 Corinthians 12:9

10. **Read Hebrews 5:2 and write down what it is saying to you.**

∞ Write out the following verses.
• Isaiah 41:10

• Isaiah 50:9

• Hebrews 13:6

11. **Write out the following verses, keeping God's power in mind.**
• 2 Chronicles 25:8

- Psalm 27:9

- Psalm 28:7

12. Look up Deuteronomy 33:29. What is the key thought here?

> How I need to bless God by speaking of His power and kingdom. How I need to order my life around one incredible thought: *God is to be honored in all I do.*[5] —*Cynthia Heald*

Dear Lord,

I thank You that You have all power. You alone can demolish strongholds and things deeply ingrained within me. I trust You to be my help, my strength in weakness, and the One who forms and shapes my heart. I look at the outside, but You go straight for the heart. O, Father, be my help for the pulling down of destructive things that would come to rob from me the life of freedom and liberty in You. Amen.

HE ENLARGES ME

Walking in Freedom While Avoiding Pitfalls and Setbacks

> If I wanted to mow my yard, I could go to the garage, take out my mower, and start pushing it in circles around my lawn. But would that get the job done?
>
> It depends. As long as the mower was working properly, my efforts would not be in vain. But what if it didn't have any gas in it? What if the spark plug wire was disconnected? What if I neglected to start it before I started mowing? Any of these problems could prevent me from doing what I had set out to do. Not only would I be working hard with no result, I would also look silly to observers. And when I finally realized what I was doing, I might feel foolish as well.[1]—*Robert McGee*

Many times well-meaning Christians just go through the motions, like someone without gas in the mower. In this lesson we will look at the work of God in our lives, and how He enlarges the borders of our hearts and minds so that we might serve Him with whole-hearted devotion. We will also look at the "gas" that we need to be fueled up and ready to go—the power of God's Spirit. Finally, we will see how prayer paves the way to a life enlarged by the presence of God, thus making us women who walk in ways, above and beyond what we think we can do . . . because of Jesus Christ. This is the way of freedom in Christ.

1. Read Romans 8:26-27.

∞ What two things does the Spirit do for you?
   1.
   2.

∞ Do you always know how to pray? Explain.

∞ Describe a time when you didn't seem to have the words that covered the prayer in your heart?

The Spirit intercedes for you according to God's will for your life—now that is a powerful truth! Prayer is a powerful tool for the Christian woman. In the previous lesson we looked at the presence of strongholds in our lives. They are a fact, and we must learn to deal with them, just as we would learn to deal with any other true and vital part of life. Now, we must understand that we must always be covered and prepared in prayer if we are going to do anything in the Spirit, whether it be intercession for others, demolishing strongholds, works of ministry and service, or carrying out our daily responsibilities.

Enlarge: *increase, boost, multiply, amplify; to make greater, expand, grow, magnify*

- Prayer connects us with God.
- Prayer tunes us in to God's purpose for us.
- Prayer is the place where we allow God to examine us and help us see where we really are standing.
- Through prayer God makes us sensitive to our true needs.
- Through prayer God enlarges us.

2. Write out Proverbs 3:5-6.

Good morning. I am God. Today I will be handling all of your problems. Please remember that I do not need your help. If life happens to deliver a situation to you that you cannot handle, do not attempt to resolve it. Kindly put it in the SFJTD (Something for Jesus To Do) box. It will be addressed in my time, not yours. Once the matter is placed into the box, do not hold on to it or remove it. Holding on or removal will delay the resolution of your problem. Because I do not sleep or slumber, there is no need for you to lose any sleep. Rest my child. If you need to contact me, I am only a prayer away.[2]

∞ What is this speaking to your life?

For me, it is saying, "Debbie, be aware of God!" It speaks to me plainly and simply that the bottom line in life is becoming more and more aware of God. My failure to acknowledge God in all my ways gets me in trouble, and then it holds me down under.

God is in the business of enlarging us. Now, ladies that doesn't mean that you are going to go up two dress sizes. It does mean, however, that He will take your heart and make it new. Your new heart will be larger and more pliable in His hands. With this new heart, you will be free to step out in larger territories of ministry and service. The largeness I am speaking about is a heart full and bursting with more of Jesus and His glorious Spirit.

∞ Look up *enlarge* in the dictionary and record the meaning here.

I like the definition that says "to reproduce something on a larger scale." It goes well with the following verse that speaks of God reproducing in us when we put our faith in him.

He is reproducing in us, to glorify the Son. He enlarges us, makes God real to others through us, in order to accomplish His work. But sometimes we just don't want God to mess with us. We think, *this is just the way I am.*

> I tell you the truth, anyone who has faith in me will do what I have been doing. He *will do even greater things* than these, because I am going to the Father. And I will do whatever you ask in my name, so that the Son may bring glory to the Father (John 14:12-13, emphasis added).

I've been this way all my life, and there's nothing I can do about it. I am not interested in changing or becoming enlarged with the Spirit of God! Satan wins battle after battle, simple because we do not stop to acknowledge God or to ask for His guidance, power, and ability.

When moving in the power of God's Spirit, we will have what we need, such as self-control and patience. We don't "try harder" to get these things, we just spend our energies filling up with Jesus. It is when we are filled with the Father that the fruit of the Spirit becomes a by-product in our lives. It is about Him, not about us. But keep in mind that in order to fill up, you must pull up to the gas tank! That is your part.

3. Read Philippians 4:4-7.

These verses contain several steps that we need to follow if our lives are going to be enlarged.

∞ What "daily living" steps do you see?

∞ What promise follows the pattern (steps) Paul gives us here?

∞ Write out Philippians 4:7.

Part of an enlarged life is having peace of mind. Peace, real inner peace, is an aspect of freedom that not many people experience.

∞ In your case, what robs you of peace?

4. Write out 1 Kings 4:29.

∞ How did God enlarge Solomon?

5. Read Genesis 17. What is the key message of this chapter?

Abraham, I am trying to tell you something—something very important. I want you to listen and to comprehend. Abraham, you were made in My image, and you were designed for a single purpose: to worship and glorify Me. . . . If you do not honor this purpose, your life will degenerate into shallow, selfish, humanistic pursuits . . . commit your whole life and future into My hands. Let Me as your Creator and God fulfill in you My perfect design. It is My great desire that you become a faithful and delighted worshiper at My throne. . . . When you have found Me, your Creator, your Redeemer and your Lord, you have found everything you need! It will be your privilege to trust and obey. It will be My privilege to bless you, guide you and sustain you!³ —*A. W. Tozer*

∞ Write out 1 Chronicles 4:10.

6. Read Isaiah 54:1-14.

∞ Write out verse 2.

∞ Read verses 1-14 again, this time out loud. Concentrate on these key points.

- Do not hold back.
- Do not be afraid.
- Do not fear disgrace.
- Remember your Redeemer, Deliverer.
- Acknowledge His "deep compassion."
- Praise Him for His "unshakable love for you."
- Stand in His righteousness.

Now . . . take on the day as a women enlarged in the power and promises of Jesus Christ.

7. What do you do with a setback?

You know the routine—you started with carrot sticks and ended with a hot fudge sundae! You promised yourself that you would change on Monday, then by Monday night, you promised you'd change on Tuesday, then by Wednesday, you promised . . . after the weekend. On and on it goes. I am not talking diet here, I am talking anything—habit, lifestyle, choices—that pulls us away from God's intended best.

∞ Ask yourself these questions, keeping in mind a recent setback in your life.

- Is this really a setback or just a slip up? Why?

- Have I opened the door for this through disobedience? How?

- Could it possibly be that I am just growing, step by step, and this is another step?

∞ Write out Colossians 2:8.

The world says, "Get it together," and you better make it quick! The message of the world is: "Shape up or ship out!" Whose message are you depending on today?

Can you trust God with a less than perfect spiritual performance? You better learn to, because, sister, no one is perfect!

When Satan wants to tempt you, he knows exactly which button to push! He knows your weaknesses as well as mine. The things that tempt you might not tempt me at all. But Satan's goal with temptation is to get all of us to live independent of God, according to the flesh rather than the Spirit.

For me, it is becoming clear that life in the Spirit needs to be my goal, not getting myself together. Every time I focus on ME, there is no fruit. When my focus is more HE, then I experience in real ways the life of the Spirit that He has planned for me to walk in.

8. **Read Ephesians 3:17-19.**

∞ What is this speaking to your heart?

∞ Read Psalm 18:16-19.

∞ What did God do for David?

∞ What was too strong for David to handle on his own? (v. 17)

∞ Who was his support?

∞ Now, write out Psalm 18:19.

∞ What does *spacious place* mean to you?

God brings us to a spacious place, an enlarged place, where we can walk in the freedom that He meant for us to walk in. Freedom from fear . . . the enemies were too strong. So what? God is the support! Freedom from going down under . . . the waters were deep. So what? God reached down from on high. Hallelujah!

∞ In what area of your life do you need God to enlarge your borders?

Do you need Him to reach down from on high today? Tell Him; He wants to help! Remember, He is everything you need!

9. Read Romans 6:1-14.

∞ Journal your thoughts on what God is speaking to your heart about an enlarged/rebuilt life.

∞ How can you offer yourself to God?

∞ What kind of instrument or vessel are you?

∞ Do you have any sin that is a master over you? Elaborate.

I am under construction and so are you. I like to think of the construction going on within me in a positive light. For many years I lived in my own little world of self-destruction. Even as a Christian I would opt for things that were destructive to my growth rather than constructive.

Self-destructive areas—where bondage commonly occurs

lusts	bad habits	loyalties	unhealthy relationships
prejudices	ambitions	duties	possessions
fears	hurts	insecurities	personal weaknesses
debts	attitudes	thoughts	unforgiveness

Take time to evaluate each area, praying for freedom in any area that is a problem for you. Allow God time to guide you through each area, revealing to you His way to freedom.

10. Write out Proverbs 16:3.

God's work produces freedom in thought, choice, speech, and action. My old life was headed toward destruction and powered by the ugly sin side of me. Now as I put that life aside, God works within me drawing me away from destruction and into a new life of positive, constructive, fruitful thoughts and deeds. But it is not by my straining, grunting, and groaning that this good stuff is happening—it is by the power of the Spirit that is at work within me.

Constructive twist on the destructive—
How the Spirit of God can turn me around

Loyalties . . . prayerful not scattered
Relationships . . . serving God, not serving self
Prejudices . . . held up to Scripture
Ambitions . . . to honor God not self
Duties . . . from compulsive to eternal aim
Debts . . . from temporal to eternal
Possessions . . . from ownership to stewardship
Security . . . in Christ instead of self-protection
Weaknesses . . . used as God's tools not Satan's bondage
Hurts . . . from resentment to God's love

11. Write out Philippians 1:6.

The book of Philippians was written by the Apostle Paul to the church he started in Philippi (Acts 16:11-40). Even though he was in prison, he felt happy when he thought of what Christ meant to him and of what the Philippians were doing for him. He gives some very practical advice on how to live the Christian life.[4]

∞ What did Paul say he was confident of in this verse? (Phil. 1:6)

∞ Do you know that Christ *completes you*? Explain.

There are two truths to sink into your heart today.
1. He began a good work in you.
2. He will complete it.

These are the types of truths that we need to marinade our minds in. Soak in the truth, let it fill you and penetrate the deepest part of you.

∞ Do you ever feel as if God is going to leave you half-finished or abandoned? Explain.

Does it feel as if things were going well for awhile, spiritual growth abounding, then plop—down, down, down into the sea of despair again, because the area that you were sure was changing has not changed but only seems to get worse? Well, you are not alone. But here Paul told the saints in Philippi: "I thank God for you, because He is working in you, and His work will be completed" (my version of Phil. 1:6). That is the bottom line. He completes you!

∞ Look up *good* in the dictionary or thesaurus, recording what you find.

∞ How does this describe the work God is doing in you right this very moment?

12. Read Philippians 1:12-21.

This passage speaks of how Paul's chains actually served to advance the Gospel. This is contrary to how we view things as modern women. We want to have a good life, feel good, get it together, and then we will be assured that God is at work within us. But Paul says that these chains were God's working, and not only God's working, but the very thing that would lead to Paul's deliverance.

∞ Does this challenge your way of thinking? How?

∞ Do you have any present chains that you thought were proof that God wasn't working in you? Elaborate.

∞ Can you turn that around now and trust God for His work? How?

∞ What is Paul's hope in the midst of his current crisis? (Phil. 1:20)

∞ What is the statement he makes about his life in verse 21?

13. Write out the following verses.
- Psalm 138:8

- Proverbs 19:21

14. Write out Philippians 2:13. *Memorize this verse.*

ॐ What does God do?

ॐ What are the two things He is getting at?
1. My _____ and
2. My _____

ॐ What is the end result of His working in you?

This verse has become a lifeline for me. It gives me such confidence to see how God is at work in me, and how He is working in my mind and emotions at the level of my "will." At that level He is putting within me the desire to act in accordance with His purposes for my life.

Have you ever just had a change of heart or attitude, and you didn't know how it happened? What about a complete reversal in desire? God is working! His Spirit is moving to get us moving according to God's will for our lives. Or have you ever come up with a "bright idea"? Did it ever occur to you that your bright idea was God's Spirit working in you, placing within your mind the very thing that would bring about God's purpose and plan in a given situation?

15. Write out the following verses.
• Ephesians 1:11

• Ephesians 2:10

• Colossians 1:29

I love the words: *"His energy, which so powerfully works in me."* When I feel that I can't do something, I can thank God for the energy that so powerfully works in me. The same energy that raised Christ from the dead is at work in me today. Wow! Think about that!

He works in each one of us for one purpose—to glorify Himself. He makes Himself real to us so that we might proclaim Him real to others. He makes Himself strong in us so that others can know His mighty strength. He rebuilds that which is broken down in us so that others can believe in a God of second chances. For it is this God of mercy who gives chance after chance to the heart that is seeking God. Oh, that God might get to the very heart of me, for the heartbeat within is the most important part of the building project.

Dear Lord,

How I thank You that You care about every part of me. You take the small parts of me and enlarge them with Your power, grace, and love. You are too good for me to even begin to understand. So, now I forget understanding and just apply simple, childlike faith to life—a life that You promised could be lived in You. Amen.

HE IS MY PURPOSE AND PASSION

Leading Me into All Truth So I May Walk in His Spirit

I have had seasons in my life when things were just not working out. In these times the easiest thing to do would be to numb my senses and pretend that all was well. It would be more comfortable to fill my life with things in an effort to distract myself, or in an effort to run far away from the place of pain. But this distraction or running would only serve to move me further from God and His purpose for my life. This is not the way of a God-confident woman, but instead it is the way of the coward.

All of us have a little coward in us. We usually do not want to experience pain. We love the Scriptures that help us understand our blessings, but we steer clear of the verses that shed light on the human condition and the sovereign purpose in pain.

We cannot be restored if we don't recognize our need. Christians often fall into the trap of thinking that they should not have feelings. In an effort to wear our faith on our sleeve instead of in the depth of our hearts, we paste on a smile, say, "Praise the Lord," and go on our merry way. Unfortunately, in the stillness of our hearts and the privacy of our homes, the way is often not merry. Many fall asleep with the nagging questions: "What is the purpose to life?" or "How can joy be restored in a life this hard?" or "How come some people are so happy?"

It is not in having feelings or problems that our passion is robbed, but it is what we choose to do with them that can throw us off course. Hardship is a part of real life. That is why understanding our purpose is vital to understanding life and moving on in our spiritual growth.

What is Our Purpose?

We were designed for relationship with God, to glorify Him with a fruitful life and to be conformed into His image. The pathway to relationship, fruitfulness, and change is not always easy. In fact, it is rarely easy because it is a pathway leading us to the end of ourselves. The Apostle Paul had a determined purpose: "I have been crucified with Christ and I no longer live, but Christ lives in me. The life I live in the body, I live by faith in the Son of God, who loved me and gave himself for me" (Gal. 2:20).

Paul lived his life passionately because he lived in faith. He also lived securely because he knew God's love for Him. When we realize that part of living for Christ is the death to self—only in dying can we finally be free to live—it is then that we live with Christ and His purposes fueling our passion for living.

In almost any current women's magazine we can find articles about passion. The passion we hear about in the media is not the passion that we learn about in Scripture. It is one thing to have a passion for quilting, design, or cooking, but it is another to have a passion to be completely God's, living passionately for His purposes.

> **Passion:**
> *enthusiasm, love, warmth, fervor, powerfully intense*

The opposite of passion is frigidity—a cold shell of a woman that is just surviving in a love-starved, faith-starved existence. In Revelation we see the church in Laodicea rebuked for being neither cold nor hot: "I wish you were either one or the other! So, because you are lukewarm—neither hot nor cold—I am about to spit you out of my mouth" (Rev. 3: 15-16).

It is obvious that God intended for us to live with passion—fervent in our love, service, and devotion to Him. Lukewarm is just a so-so existence. We live lukewarm lives when we do not deal with reality, do not deal with the truth, and do not have faith in our God.

Happiness is not dependent on happenings, but on the relationship that persists in that happening. When we act on the Word of God, and not on our feelings, we experience that God means His promises. The fact is that God watches over His Word to perform it.[1]
—*Corrie Ten Boom*

The point in this lesson will be to learn what it means to live in the fullness of what Christ has provided for us. In times when we would rather depend on numbed senses than God, He says, "My daughter, come to me."

If like me, you have found yourself in times of wondering what life is really all about, you need help. It is in the times of personal struggle for significance, meaning, and happiness that we need to go to THE Wonderful Counselor. We have been given a wonderful God. We must now go to the source that has already been given to us—first, not last! (Jesus, Wonderful Counselor). If I don't go to Jesus and His Spirit first, I will run around like a chicken with my head cut off! But, if I go to the Father and ask for His counsel and help, He will guide me into all truth for my personal life. He knows exactly what I need to match my circumstances with healing.

This may mean He leads me to a trusted friend, pastor, or professional. Many times another can help us have courage to face a painful situation, but if the advice given is contrary to the Word of God, we are just getting bound in more chains and developing more problems then we started with. If you go for outside help, find a believer who will lead you straight to the truth of God's precepts and principles. Daughter of God, Jesus wants every part of you, and He will lead you and guide you into all truth when you *go to Him*! He is the one who has been with you every day of your life, in every breath that you've taken, and in every crisis that you faced. He knows you inside and out. Wouldn't it make sense to seek counsel from the God who set all things in motion, created the earth and everything in it, and most of all has divine power to heal?

> **Counselor:**
> *adviser, mentor,*
> *consultant*

1. **Read Psalm 16:7-11.**

∞ Who counsels you?

∞ Who is set before you?

∞ Will you be confident? (not shaken) Why?

∞ What is made known to you?

> *I am the LORD your God, who teaches you what is best for you, who directs you in the way you should go (Isa. 48:17).*

I love the fact that God ministers to me and counsels me even while I sleep. We worry so much about things that we just need to give to God. He will advise us and lead us if we will rely on Him. How amazing to think that He can even advise us in our sleep!

2. **Write out Proverbs 12:15 and Proverbs 13:10.**

In order to have fellowship with each other, we must first have fellowship with the Father. This is where some Christians fall into huge traps and wonder why their church relationships are sour.

∞ How do you listen to God?

3. **Write out the following verses.**
   • Isaiah 30:19-21

> Advice: *a piece of information given about what to do or how to behave*

   • 2 Timothy 3:16

∞ What do these verses say that challenges you to apply the Word of God in your life?

4. **Read Psalm 119.**
   Concentrate on the instruction to "meditate" on God's Word. There are ten references to meditation just in this psalm alone.

∞ What is this speaking to your heart?

Meditate: *to think deeply and quietly, to set one's mind upon something*

When I meditate on something, sitting with a thought for a time, it goes into my heart and usually affects my actions. If it is God's truth that I am thinking of and sitting with, His Word becomes alive and begins to affect my daily experience. I think this would be called going from head to heart.

∞ Write out Luke 6:45.

∞ What comes out of us is overflow. What is stored in your heart today? Would if be beneficial or fruitful if it spilled out? Explain.

5. Write out Psalm 119:24.

God's statues are His precepts, the instruction in His Word. His Word counsels us.

6. Write out Psalm 119:45.

∞ When will we walk in freedom?

True freedom comes when we discover God's purpose in our life. We look for external purpose first, when we should be looking to a deeper purpose that comes from the very core of who we are. God created us to know Him and to make Him known.

I know Him by reading His Word, communicating with Him in constant thought and prayer, and by walking with Him in daily surrender. I make Him known by bearing fruit as I abide in His power. He is made known as He is poured through my life to others.

> I often ask myself the question, "Why do I get up I the morning?" In answering this question, I am reminded daily that my purpose is to get up, set my heart, mind, and soul before the Lord, and walk through the day trusting in His grace and yielding to His plan for my life. This is easy to write, but not easy to do. I don't like life when I'm hurt, when people won't do what I think they should do, when people I love make wrong decisions, when I'm denied what I think is best. As I look at this last sentence, it is full of "I's." That is the key to understanding my purpose—it is not my purpose or my life—it is God's purpose and God's life. I don't want to just "make it through life trying to grab or manipulate a little peace and happiness." I want the very best that God has to offer while I am here, and I want to offer Him my very best, no matter what my circumstances might be.
>
> I want to stay focused on the things that are eternal: God, Himself, His Word, and people. I want my abiding to grow deeper and deeper so that as others observe my life, they will give glory to God. I want to have the compassion and boldness of Christ in relating to others.[2] —*Cynthia Heald*

7. **What is Christ called in Isaiah 9:6?**

∞ Do you think He can counsel you? What do you need advice on today?

8. Read Romans 11:33-36.

∞ What is this saying to you?

∞ Would you accept counsel from One who has depth and riches of wisdom? Explain.

Peace in Trusting His Counsel

9. Write out the following verses.
  • Isaiah 26:3-4

  • Isaiah 26:12

Remember God and His Purposes

10. Read the following and write out the key thoughts.
  • Psalm 33:10-11

  • Proverbs 19:21

  • Isaiah 46:9-13

> You are on the road to success if you realize that failure is only a detour. In order to realize the worth of the anchor, we need to feel the stress of the storm. When a train goes through a tunnel and it gets dark, you don't throw away your ticket and jump off. You sit still and trust the engineer. Our trust and hope are not in the promises, but in the One who made the promises. Our faith may falter, but His faithfulness, never![3] —*Corrie Ten Boom*

He Formed You

11. Write out the following verses, personalizing them in your heart.
  • Psalm 33:15

  • Psalm 33:22

12. Read the following verses and journal on their meaning to you today.
  • Isaiah 45:12

  • Isaiah 46:3-4

  • Ephesians 1:11

Counseled to Walk in the Spirit

13. Once again read Galatians 5:16-25, outlining the practical instructions that can be applied to your life today.

Early one morning I was thinking about this verse . . . keep in step with the Spirit. With music blaring in my early morning step aerobics class and the frustrated instructor eyeing me as the black sheep of the group, I wondered how I would ever make it through the routine. All the steps seemed foreign to me. Even the basic steps threw me off-balance if I was not in sync with the music and if I was not attentive to the instructor. Still up and down I went, trying to fit in the fancy footwork and choreographed arm movements.

> *Since we live by the Spirit, let us keep in step with the Spirit (Gal. 5:25).*

I began to notice something that reminded me of the Galatians 5:25 verse. As I keep focused on the instructor's routine and movements, I lost myself in following the routine and finishing the class. For that moment in time exercising didn't seem so hard. So it is with my spiritual life. It is when I keep focused on the moving of God's Spirit, my instructor, that I lose myself in following the leading of God. Life suddenly seems manageable. Pretty soon it isn't about me anymore, but about following the lead of an all-wise teacher.

When I take my focus off the teacher, I miss a beat, lose a step, and stumble and fall. Often I can barely get up before I've missed another beat and fall again. Without a clear focus, I realize I would never finish the class. And in real life, I know I won't finish the race, the journey set before me, without a clear focus on God.

The Spirit of God is our life, our teacher, counselor, and guide. We live by the Spirit of God working within us. Since this is true, it is important that I keep in step with the beat of the Spirit rather than the beat of my own plans and agendas. In doing so, I will most definitely finish the class, finish the race, and feel refreshed when this day's routine is over.

> *But the Counselor, the Holy Spirit, whom the Father will send in my name, will teach you all things and will remind you of everything I have said to you (John 14:26, emphasis added).*

14. Write out John 14:26.

∞ What is the job of the Holy Spirit?

∞ What will He teach you?

There were days when I had so much emotional baggage that it seemed as if I needed bellhops to help me carry it around! But, since there were no bellhops or other attendants to help me with the load, I carried it alone. Filled with hurt, fear, and insecurity, I trudged along each day, dragging behind me all of my troubles. On the outside I tried to be a brave, strong Christian, but my troubled heart was too big for me to understand and too broken for me to fix. I needed a counselor!

I spent time working on all of my "stuff." At times the load seemed to lighten, but then the heaviness would come to greet me again with the morning sun. Though I worked through the steps to wholeness, I wasn't resembling "whole." Most of me remained broken and confused. I needed to put my hope in God, not in human wisdom.

Fortunately there were people who helped me stay focused on Christ and the truth about life, through some traumatic life events. They directed me to put my hope in God, living one day at a time, while also acknowledging where I needed healing and wholeness. No more denial . . . Jesus knew my heart, knew my circumstances, knew my problems, and desired to lead me to solutions and hope, as well as to spiritual and emotional health.

Together we moved through points of pain—me and my Maker. I began relying on the power of the Holy Spirit to do exactly what God said He would do—counsel me, teach me, direct me, and guide me. I had gone through several life changes at one time. My stress level in the life experience department was "off the chart!" On all accounts,

> *Then you will know that I am the LORD; those who hope in me will not be disappointed (Isa. 49:23).*

I should have been having a complete breakdown. Some days I was so depressed that I could hardly get out of bed. Seeking another to walk alongside of me helped me navigate through the rough waters of life in a God-honoring way.

For years prior to this I was finding myself increasingly discouraged as I went the self-help route and realized that it would take forever to straighten out my messed-up path. I felt as if I was going nowhere! It seemed as if I would have to work on "me" and make that my focus for a long, long time. I was not comfortable with that.

Then I discovered that *in making God my focus* and recognizing Him as my counselor and healer a lifetime of baggage began emptying out, little by little. The suitcases were transferred to another plane. The Lord was taking all my broken pieces, and the Holy Spirit was leading and guiding me into all truth. It is God who does the miracle of restoration by restoring both purpose and passion in the human heart. He pulled me out of the pit of despair and depression. I know He has the power to do this for anyone who will honestly seek Him, being real and open before God with all the broken pieces of the heart.

If it's free, it's advice

If you pay for it, it's counseling

If it works, it's a miracle!

Only God can do the impossible—a miraculous and lasting change.

It is amazing what clarity God can give us regarding our life and all the various pains and hang-ups we experience. Sometimes we keep our old selves attached to us like baggage claim tickets. We don't need a claim ticket to remind us of all our shortcomings and failures. Give the ticket over to God. Thank Him for the clarity of mind He gives when we go to Him for guidance and truth. Holding onto your old "claim tickets" only keeps you locked in the past and focused on yourself and your pain. Don't deny your pain. Denial keeps you stuck and keeps you living as a victim. Bring your pain to God in personal, conversational prayer. Truth and honesty bring victory and freedom.

Faith sees the invisible, believes the unbelievable, and receives the impossible.[5]— Corrie Ten Boom

Have you had a less than perfect life? Get real with it, deal with it, give it to God, and learn from your life experience. Keep in mind that part of God's purpose for us is change. Change happens when we are rearranged. All of life's variables have the capacity to rearrange and change us. Embrace Christ in the pain of your changing life and be set free to live fully. In faith move on to new chapters of life, new living in Him. Don't stay stuck in your past; it is over. Deal with the pain, take it to the Father, and move into tomorrow with grace and truth. You probably won't "feel" better right away. You may even live through a season of pain while you are learning to trust and let go. Keep abiding in Christ. He will deliver you and restore you.

God the Father did a wonderful thing for us. He gave us His Spirit to live in us, dwell with us, and teach us all things! Not too many of us take advantage of the great resource of wisdom and insight that is residing within us each day.

It is the assignment of the Holy Spirit to be our counselor and to teach us all things and to bring to our remembrance every purpose and intent of Jesus Christ.

∞ Are you taking God up on His plan of counsel and wisdom? How?

∞ Are you opening yourself up to be trained by the Spirit of Christ? How?

Think today of the Holy Spirit as being your personal instructor. He is your personal teacher, trainer, coach, and counselor. And just think, you get to read the very breath of God each time you open the Bible and take in the truth on the pages before you!

When you rely on God's Spirit in this way, you are really experiencing an encounter with the Almighty God and counselor Himself. He knows your pain, and He is the Healer! He knows the blueprint for your life, and He gives you purpose. He has gifted you in ways untouched and possibly unknown by you, and He alone unlocks passion.

God's love for us is not conditional. It is fixed. He is committed to loving those He created. He is committed to empowering those who come to Him through Jesus Christ. It is the power of God's love and grace that restores and changes lives. Nothing is impossible to God! As we come to Him, He will shine His light through us into the dark and dying world we live in. Oh that we might find restoration through Christ's life in us, actively working and moving in us, His children.

Dear Lord,

How wonderful that You are my personal guide in this life. Thank You for giving me Your Spirit, to instruct, guide, counsel, land comfort me. Your love is often too big for me even to pretend to understand. You thought of everything! I ask You now to give me clarity in areas that need healing and deliverance. Lord, be my healer, my helper, my teacher, leading me through the maze of life. Today I want to leave the baggage at Your claim center and approach the rest of my trip with unencumbered freedom. Amen.

HE REMAINS FAITHFUL

Learning to Rest in What Is True about God, Life, and Myself

> *But you, O Sovereign LORD, deal well with me for your name's sake; out of the goodness of your love, deliver me (Ps. 109:21).*

God Rules! It's a fashionable bumper sticker, but do we know what the message "God rules" implies, and do we believe that it is true?

To rule means to have governing authority, as a sovereign.

To be sovereign means to reign supreme, to have all authority and power.

Does God have the reigns of your life today?

Are His power and authority operative in your life?

It may seem as if He isn't too supreme on your behalf as you look at all the circumstances that keep crowding out your joy. Do you wonder if He is really the faithful One that you keep hearing He is?

Men have to go through many experiences in order to get the spiritual vision which is needed to see the divine plan. A film is always developed in a dark room.[1] —*Corrie Ten Boom*

God is sovereign, and whether you realize it or not He is ruling in your life and dealing well with you. Why? Because of His love just for you.

Out of the goodness of His love, He deals with us and delivers us from all the wounds inflicted on us from the battleground of real life. He knows we aren't waltzing through a rose garden each day. He knows that life gets hard and that we face difficulties, which often hurt us deeply. He knows our frame.

As strong as we'd like to think we are, the truth is that we are all poor and needy. Poor in spirit when we face disappointment, needy of heart when we are emotionally wounded and left to die. No, we aren't strong by ourselves, but, we are strong in the strength of this mighty sovereign Lord that is here today offering healing, hope, and deliverance. Yes . . . God Rules! You can count on it!

In this lesson we will be looking at what it means to have an attitude of thanksgiving, an attitude of gratitude—which is focusing our hearts on God's faithfulness. We are encouraged to turn our hearts towards home, our real home, and live as if eternity is real—because it is.

Turning Your Heart toward Home

My phone rings endlessly, and I've been blessed with many friends. My mailbox is often plump with thoughtful cards and notes. So how, with wonderful people surrounding me, could I ever feel a long, lonely distance between myself and others? Yet at times I do.

Loneliness for me is like a dull ache, a sadness, a feeling of being forgotten. It feels as if I'm calling for help down a long, empty hall. When I'm lonely, I feel misunderstood, neglected and separate. I'm then a prime candidate for self-pity to come visiting. Actually, it's more than a visit, for self-pity brings her endless supply of tissues and becomes a sniveling houseguest, uninvited yet indulged.

How is it that so many people (6 billion) live on earth, and yet longitudes are one of our greatest emotional and relational battles?

Could it be that loneliness began when Adam and Eve opted to go their own way? I wonder if the ache within could be a call to our hearts to turn toward Home? Perhaps loneliness is a scary siren to remind us that people are unable, try as they might, to move close enough to ease our deep discomfort and disconnection. If that's so, is it possible that loneliness is actually an evangelist, a teacher, even a friend?[2] —*Patsy Clairmont*

Those words from the book *Sportin' a 'Tude* are a reminder to me that I need to develop an attitude of remembering the faithfulness of God. He is to be my closest friend and daily confidant. This attitude needs to permeate everything I do, color everything I see, and remind me that my sufficiency and freedom is only in Christ.

Yes, I must turn my *heart towards Home.* Together let's switch gears, turning our hearts towards Home and learning to rest in what is true about God, life, and ourselves. As we allow God to fill our every need, our every longing, and our every loneliness, we will be free, beautiful, confident women of God.

> Faithful:
> *loyal, trustworthy,*
> *true to the facts,*
> *steadfast, fixed,*
> *firm, unchanging*

1. Read Psalm 25. Underline verses that speak to your heart.

∞ What are some of those verses? Explain what they mean to you personally.

David had a lot going on. He seemed to have troubles on every side. But he still continually reverted to a focus on God.

> *My eyes are ever on*
> *the LORD, for only*
> *He will release my*
> *feet from the snare*
> *(Ps. 25:15).*

Here once again we see the picture of a child of God trusting in God's power to redeem and deliver him from the power of all the "stuff" in the path. Only God can release me from the things that snare me. Only God can redeem me from the death that comes from living for myself, and only God can take away my sins as well as my loneliness.

∞ Write out Psalm 25:22.

2. Read Psalm 130.
∞ What are the two things the psalmist does in verse 5?
   1.
   2.

∞ Write out verses 7-8.

3. Read 1 Peter 4:1-4.

What a great picture. Christ suffered—it cost Him something to buy me back. But in buying me back from the darkness of this world and the deceitfulness of my flesh, He set me free to live for Him—that is why Christ is my redeemer. Now I can live my life for the will of God. What a relief when life has a purpose, and when that purpose is much, much bigger than I am.

I am redeemed.

I have everything I need, in Christ.

4. Read Deuteronomy 7:6-9.

The Children of Israel were entering a land filled with pagan worship. They had already experienced the wrath of God when they allowed themselves to be seduced by the Moabites (see Num. 25). Now their personal obedience to God was more important than ever. Moses gives them motives to obey. He points out that they belong to God and that God is faithful.

As you read the passage in Deuteronomy 7, put yourself in the place of the Israeltites. Surely you too are in a land filled with pagan practices—just look around. In light of that, answer the following questions.

∞ Why did the Lord set His affection on you?

∞ What are you called when you are His?

Because the Sovereign LORD helps me, I will not be disgraced. Therefore have I set my face like flint, and I know I will not be put to shame (Isa. 50:7).

∞ From what did He redeem you?

5. Read the remainder of Deuteronomy 7.

Because we have been chosen to be God's, we are to remain fully His just as the Israelites needed to be set apart and fully His. He will bless us as we walk with Him. We are not to serve other gods . . . people, money, beauty, success, things . . . nothing but God. He will redeem us with His mighty power and hand, keeping us from being consumed with things that will keep us from knowing Him. Some are afraid to let go of the world; they hold on tightly to what they know. What they know is comfortable. But God says not to be afraid, because He is a great and awesome God. We are not to covet what the world lives for—it will be a trap for us! We have been redeemed and set apart for Him.

∞ What are your thoughts on this? What can you take away from this lesson that can be applied to your real and everyday life?

Let's Review

6. God is faithful to deliver you.

Do you want Calgon to take you away? Have you noticed that life is not a cakewalk? Did you remember that He said He is everything?

∞ What is God called in Isaiah 9:6?
  1.
  2.
  3.
  4.

Do you know He is the keeper of your welfare, the Prince of Peace?

∞ Write out Psalm 18:17.

∞ Write out 2 Peter 1:3.

∞ What has He given you? Who is He?

> Slow me down, Lord.
> I am going too fast.
> I can't see my brother
> When he is going past.
>
> I miss a lot of good things
> Day by Day.
> I can't see a blessing
> When it comes my way.[3]
> —*Corrie Ten Boom*

7. God is faithful to redeem you.

∞ Remember my little chair, once stripped of all that old yucky paint? What did it become?

∞ Write out Jeremiah 29:11.

∞ What are three things God has for you?
  1.
  2.
  3.

∞ Write out Romans 3:23.

∞ Write out Romans 5:7-8.

8. He is faithful to set you free.
Are you held down and back? Remember who He is!

∞ Write out John 8:32.

∞ Write out John 8:36.

∞ Read again 1 Corinthians 13:11-13. What are you to leave behind?

9. He is faithful to define you.

∞ Do you live in your new identity? Explain.

∞ Write out Galatians 2:20.

∞ Read 2 Corinthians 5:16-17. What do these verses say about God, life, and you?

Because of our position in Christ, great things are true of us. It is in focusing on what is true that we can begin to have joy in the fact that we are new creatures, new people when we are in Christ!

If you are a believer, you can say the following about yourself. [4]

> I have peace with God (Rom. 5:1).
> I am accepted by God (Eph. 1).
> I am a child of God (John 1:12).
> I am indwelt by the Holy Spirit (1 Cor. 3:16).
> I have access to God's wisdom (James 1:5).
> I am helped by God (Heb. 4:16).
> I am reconciled to God (Rom. 5:11).
> I have no condemnation (Rom. 8:1).
> I am justified (Rom. 5:1).
> I am His representative (2 Cor. 5:20).
> I am completely forgiven (Col. 1:14).
> I have my needs met by God (Phil. 4:19).
> I am tenderly loved (Jer. 31:1).
> I am the temple of God (1 Cor. 3:16).

10. He is faithful to be your courage in a less than perfect world.

☞ Are you operating in the chains of pain? Explain.

☞ Read 2 Corinthians 1:3-6 out loud. How does having a "so that" mentality help you see the purpose in some of life's pain?

☞ Read Philippians 3:12-21. What does this speak to your free heart today?

Courage is fear that has said its prayers.[5] —*Corrie Ten Boom*

11. He is faithful to be your strength.

⊚ Write out Philippians 4:13.

⊚ Where does your strength come from today?

⊚ What can you do?

⊚ Why can you do it?

12. He is faithful to rebuild you.

⊚ Read Psalm 51:10-12.
⊚ What four restoration qualities (vv. 10, 12) does the psalmist pray for?

⊚ Who is to do the rebuilding (note v. 11)? Considering the nature of these four qualities, why might that be contrary to what most would expect?

13. He is faithful to work in you.

⊚ Write out Philippians 2:13.

God begins working in our will—at mind level. The result of such a work is that we live according to His purpose. He works in us, makes us willing, and completes His purposes through His people.

14. He is faithful to help you.

∞ Read Hebrews 4:15-16.

∞ How is Christ characterized in these verses?

∞ What is He able to do for you?

15. He is faithful to enlarge you.

∞ Write out Psalm 146:3.

16. He is faithful to give you a purpose for living.

When we understand our loving Father, our hearts come alive with a passion to serve Him. He becomes our purpose, His plans our joy and delight. It is His love that moves us to this type of surrender and purpose.

∞ Read 2 Corinthians 5:14-15. What in life compelled the Apostle Paul?

∞ Look up the definition of *compel*.

∞ Has the love of God influenced your life? If so, how?

∞ What purpose did Paul say he was going to live for?

17. He is faithful to be faithful to His children.

∞ Read Hebrews 11:6. What do you need in order to please God?

∞ Write out Hebrews 11:1—the definition of faith.

∞ According to Hebrews 11:6 what are two things must you believe about God?
1.
2.

∞ Would holding these two truths in your heart make a difference in your life personally? Explain.

In closing, I want us to be reminded of the fact that all we are, and all we are able to do, are a direct result of the faithfulness of Almighty God. Stop now, and go some place where you can be alone. For some of you, that might be the bathroom, others might just have to pull the apron over your head and pretend to be alone. Nevertheless, get alone with God . . . somewhere, somehow.

Why? Because you need to praise Him for who He is, thank Him for what He has done, submit to Him every part of you, and sing a new song for HE HAS SET YOU FREE.

Don't be like the woman who thought she was poor when she was actually rich. She didn't acknowledge that her parents left her a million dollars when they died. She was told, but for some reason, she just didn't let it sink in,

> Be sure you remain covered with a canopy of praise. It is like a tent over and around you. Satan has no entrance as long as you pin down the sides by praising, and thank God for His wonderful promises. In the life of the true believer there are no accidents.[6]—*Corrie Ten Boom*

and she lived as if she didn't know the facts. She died herself a poor woman, but actually, she was rich; the money was left untouched in her account!

You, precious woman, are rich. You have received a divine inheritance. Jesus has already deposited in your account. Now, daily draw all that you need, and praise Him for His provision. Believe it, for He has already bought your freedom!

> From the LORD comes deliverance. May your blessing be on your people (Ps. 3:8).

Dear Lord,

Thank You for Your restoring love and all that Your love and care accomplishes in my life. Thank You for Your faithfulness, Your blessing, and also for the times of darkroom developing . . . long dark times that are necessary. May I always have courage, always seek You, always believe that You are everything! Oh that I may daily depend on You and Your restoring love . . . a love so sweet, a love so faithful, a love so real that it touches upon even the deepest part of me, setting me free! Lord, may I live completely for You and Your purposes. Amen.

ENDNOTES

Two: He Redeems Me
1 Robert McGee, *The Search for Freedom* (Ann Arbor, Mich.: Vine Books, 1995), p. 83.
2 Ibid., p. 52.
3 A.W. Tozer, *Gems from Tozer* (Camp Hill, Pa.: Christian Publications, 1969), 29.

Three: He Sets Me Free
1 Max Lucado, "The Applause of Heaven," in *Life Lessons/Hebrews* (Nashville: Word Publishing, 1997), p. 71.
2 Robert McGee, *Search for Freedom*, p. 25.
3 Dr. Verle Bell, *True Freedom* (Ann Arbor, Mich.: Vine Books, 1993), p. 72.

Four: He Defines Me
1 "Notes on John 10:10," *Life Application Study Bible* (Wheaton, Ill.: Tyndale House Publishers, 1996).

Five: He Is My Courage
1 William Backus and Marie Chapian, *Telling Yourself the Truth*, (Minneapolis: Bethany House Publishers, 1980), p. 17.
2 Steve McVay, *Grace Walk* (Eugene, Ore.: Harvest House Publishers, 1995), p. 32.
3 H. Norman Wright, *Your Tomorrows Can Be Different from Your Yesterdays* (Grand Rapids, Mich.: Fleming H. Revell Co., 1995), pp. 69-70.
4 Corrie Ten Boom, *Jesus Is Victor* (Grand Rapids, Mich.: Fleming H. Revell Co., 1977), p. 147.
5 Backus and Chapian, *Telling Yourself the Truth*, p. 25.
6 Ibid., p. 21.
7 Corrie Ten Boom, *Jesus Is Victor*, p. 170.

Six: He Is My Strength
1 Max Lucado, "He Still Moves Stones," in *Life Lessons/Hebrews* (Nashville: Word Publishing, 1997), p. 38.
2 Steve McVay, *Grace Walk*, 32.

Seven: He Rebuilds Me
1 H. Norman Wright, *Your Tomorrows Can Be Different from Your*

Yesterdays, p. 126.
2 Dr. Verle Bell, *True Freedom*, p. 18.
3 Cynthia Heald, *Becoming a Woman of Purpose* (Colorado Springs: NavPress, 1994), p. 52.

Eight: He Works in Me
1 Max Lucado, *Just Like Jesus* (Nashville: Word Publishing, 1998), pp. 3-4.
2 Leonard Felder, *A Fresh Start* (New York: Signet Books, 1987) adapted from p. 8 of H. Norman Wright, *Your Tomorrows Can Be Different from Your Yesterdays*.

Nine: He Is My Help
1 Beth Moore, *Praying God's Word* (Nashville: Broadman and Holman, 2000), p. 6.
2 Robert McGee, *Search for Freedom*, p. 101.
3 Beth Moore, *Praying God's Word*, p. 3.
4 Robert McGee, *Search for Freedom*, p. 101.
5 Cynthia Heald, *Becoming a Woman of Purpose*, p. 14.

Ten: He Enlarges Me
1 Robert McGee, *Search for Freedom*, p. 161.
2 Author unknown. Search the internet for "SFJTD" to locate several sources.
3 A.W. Tozer, *Men Who Met God* (Camp Hill, Pennsylvania: Christian Publications, 1986), pp. 23-25.
4 "Study Notes," *Women's Devotional Bible*, p. 1,306.

Eleven: He Is My Purpose and Passion
1 Corrie Ten Boom, *Jesus Is Victor*, 153.
2 Cynthia Heald, *Becoming a Woman of Purpose*, p. 94.
3 Corrie Ten Boom, *Jesus Is Victor*, p. 183.

Twelve: He Remains Faithful
1 Corrie Ten Boom, *Jesus Is Victor*, p. 184.
2 Patsy Clairmont, *Sportin' a 'Tude* (Colorado Springs: Focus on the Family, 1996), p. 105.
3 Corrie Ten Boom, *Jesus Is Victor*, p. 153.
4 Josh McDowell, *His Image, My Image* (San Bernadino, California: Here's Life Publishing, pp. 198, 101.
5 Corrie Ten Boom, *Jesus Is Victor*, p. 177.
6 Ibid.

Reasonable care has been taken to trace ownership of the materials quoted from in this book, and to obtain permission to use copyrighted materials, when necessary.

A Personal Note From the **Author**

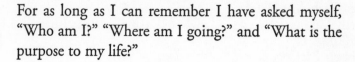

More than to just entertain, Cook publishing hopes to inspire you to fulfill the great commandment: to love God with all your heart, soul, mind, and strength; and your neighbor as yourself. Towards that end, the author wishes to share these personal thoughts with you.

Heart

For as long as I can remember I have asked myself, "Who am I?" "Where am I going?" and "What is the purpose to my life?"

I grew up trying to find purpose in the approval and acceptance of others. In the process of living for approval, I lost myself. It's a bit embarassing to admit that as a Christian woman I longed for the acceptance of others instead of longing for God. My identity was wrapped up in people, titles, family, ministry, and things. I couldn't tell you who I was, only what I did. After going through a life crisis, I was forced to reevaluate everything I ever believed in. I spent months concentrating only on what was true in God's Word, reestablishing myself and my foundation in mind-renewing, life-transforming truth.

What has emerged is a woman who has found out who she is and where she is going and a woman who has peace and a new found confidence in God's love and joy. As I step back and think of where I have been, I thank God for His restoring love in my life. It is because of His love that I have been set free to live for Him!

Soul

King David said of His God, "The Lord is my shepherd; I shall not want" (Ps. 23:1, KJV). I have found great comfort in grasping the tender love of God for me and the care that follows me all the days of my life. I have learned to sit with truths from God's Word, meditating on them, personalizing them, digesting them . . . making them mine. As I have sat with the Truth, my mind has been made new, my life has been turned upside down, and my faith in God taken to new heights.

Yes, I shall not want, for God knows all that I have need of. He feeds me, leads me, guides me, and protects me. That is what a good shepherd does.

Mind

You may notice that you have unhealthy thought patterns. You are not alone; all of us have thought patterns that need to be renewed in the truth of God's Word. I have found *Praying God's Word*, by Beth Moore, exceptionally helpful in dealing with mental strongholds by providing the Scripture necessary to build up my heart and lead me in praying according to Scripture.

If your battlefield is insecurity and fear, I encourage you to work through the pages of my study *Steadfast Love: Finding Self-worth Through God's Truth*. If you have trouble letting go of hurt, bitterness, and other relational problems, I encourage you to use *Living Love: The Choice that Can Change Your Heart*. I also recommend *The Velveteen Woman*, by Brenda Waggoner, on your journey to becoming whole and real. This book is a true delight.

Strength

I hope that you take the time necessary to process what God is speaking to your heart. Though this study can be done devotionally, getting together with another to discuss the way God is touching our lives through His Word is motivating and inspiring. I know of women who keep in touch across the miles doing a study together via e-mail, pouring out on their computer screen all that God is showing them. The personal accountability provides a place for us to gain strength from each other.

If this study helps you let go of past hurts, old messages, and distracting thoughts—while replacing them with God's Word—the purpose of Restoring Love will be accomplished. Take the time to allow freedom in Christ to take hold of you! And while you are held in His embrace, may you discover true passion and purpose for living!

Dear Lord, I ask you to make yourself real to each woman who works through the pages of this book. May she find strength and help as she goes to your Word for real-life answers. May she find that you are her everything: her counselor, her redeemer, her courage, her deliverer, and the restorer of her soul. I pray that each of us, as your women, will find our life's purpose in you. Give us the grace to live one day at a time, experiencing the gift of the present. And may we live each present day to glorify you.

Debbie Alsdorf